Redemptive Responses of Jesus

REDEMPTIVE RESPONSES OF JESUS

HOWARD W. ROBERTS

BROADMAN PRESS
Nashville, Tennessee

Library of Congress Cataloging-in-Publication Data

Roberts, Howard W., 1947-
    Redemptive responses of Jesus.

    Bibliography: p.
    1. Jesus Christ—Biography—Public life.
2. Jesus Christ—Adversaries.   3. Jesus Christ—
Influence.   4. Christian biography—Palestine.
I. Title.
BT340.R64   1987   232.9'03   86-12897
ISBN 0-8054-5715-1

To Peggy, who has made
exploring life with her for
more than twenty years of my life
a joy beyond description and who, more
than anyone else in my life, has helped me
to admit my anger, to face it constructively,
and to discover ways to use my anger redemptively.

.

Contents

Introduction 9

1. Responding to Anger 11

2. Responding to Hypocrisy 27

3. Responding to Prejudice 45

4. Responding to Rejection 70

5. Responding to Charlantry 89

6. Responding to Denial 107

7. Responding to Betrayal 123

Bibliography 139

Introduction

The life of Jesus continues to intrigue me. As a pastor for the past twenty years I have found myself examining and reexamining the life of Jesus to find direction for my life and to discover insight that would be helpful to people in their own life struggles. What I have found in Jesus is the divine Son sent from God who knew well how to be a human being. All of us were created and called to be human beings. Examining the life of Jesus will aid us to close the gap between potential and performance in our lives.

As I explore the biblical accounts of Jesus' life, I am amazed again and again at the responses that Jesus made to people as He encountered them. He let His feelings show. He told stories that were funny to the point of tears, that is a person with a two-by-four sticking out of his or her own eye attempting to get a splinter out of another's eye. He enjoyed parties, that is the wedding feast in Cana, but people accused Him of excessive eating and drinking. He developed close friends, that is Mark wrote that He called His disciples to be with Him. He was disappointed by His friends, that is in Gethsemane He said to three of them, "Could you not watch with me one hour?" (Matt. 26:40). He cried when Lazarus died. And Jesus got angry.

That Jesus got angry surprises a lot of us who at some time have equated anger with sin. Few can read the account of Jesus chasing the money changers out of the Temple without admitting that Jesus was angry, but many refuse to see anger any other time in Jesus' life. Jesus cured a man's hand on the sabbath, and people wanted to accuse Him of doing wrong. Mark wrote that Jesus looked at them with anger (3:5). Jesus was angered whenever and wherever He saw people being treated unfairly and unjustly.

Motivated by His care and compassion for people, yet angered when He saw people being mistreated, Jesus responded redemptively to people in those situations. This book is about Jesus, people, and some of the redemptive responses that Jesus made to those who were being unjust and unfair. Jesus' responses were redemptive because His intention clearly was to bring people into a healthy, wholesome relationship with God and with each other.

This book is about us. It is about times when we are unjust and unfair to others. It is about ways we can respond redemptively to them. As we learn from Christ to respond redemptively to other persons, we will discover ourselves becoming a part of the redeeming people of God. That is what we are called to be when God invites us to be partners with Him. The best way we can sing of our Redeemer is to join with others in being redeeming people.

1
Responding to Anger

Matthew 5: 21-26, 38-48

Jesus was a human being, but we have difficulty believing it. Many of us want to major on Jesus' deity as though He was not also human. The time span between His life and ours is only a minor struggle. Our major struggle with believing Jesus was a human being is that we have to forfeit our alibis for our poor showings as people. Jesus is the model of wholeness for all persons, but our lives reveal that much of His modeling has been lost on us.

For many years Jesus was portrayed as an emotionless person, which are mutually exclusive words. People today accept a partially emotional Jesus. They agree that He expressed love and joy. They have some difficulty accepting Jesus' humor, and, except for cleansing the Temple, they strongly resist the idea that Jesus got angry. The Gospel writers, however, did not hesitate to record the anger of Jesus.

Anger's Countenance

There is adequate guidance in the Bible about anger. The ancient Hebrews knew of it and identified its presence in the first family by recording that Cain became angry with Abel and that his countenance fell. The face is the place where the message of one's life is read. Paul Ekman, an expert on the human face, has developed the facial action coding system to register the role of facial muscles in expressing human emotions. Ekman explains that the tightening of muscle 23 results in a narrowing of the lips, which is an early sign of anger.[1] This was the Hebrews' understanding of how God knew Cain was angry.

11

"The Lord said to Cain, 'Why are you angry, and why has your countenance fallen?' " (Gen. 4:6).

The problem for Cain was not that he became angry but that his anger made him vulnerable. As the biblical writer recorded "Sin is couching at the door; its desire is for you, but you must master it" (v. 7). We are not told why Cain's offering was unacceptable. Could it have been what Jesus later suggested, that if you come to the altar and remember that your brother has something against you, you are to leave your offering, go to be reconciled with your brother, and then return to give your offering? Whatever the reason for Cain's offering not being accepted, his self-worth was threatened, anger was evoked, and it showed in his face.

The instructional warning was *not:* "Don't get angry." Cain had no control over whether he would get angry or not. The warning was that he not allow his anger to motivate him to sinful action. He needed to master the urges, desires, and options that the anger stimulated rather than permit them to master him. One of the desires that arises when people are threatened is to destroy whatever or whoever represents the threat. Thus Cain killed Abel who symbolized threat to him. Although threats are internal, many follow Cain's lead and seek an external solution to this internal problem.

Nursing Anger

Jesus gave guidance about anger in the Sermon on the Mount. With six examples He illustrated how the law of His kingdom fulfilled and, therefore, superceded the Mosaic law (Matt: 5:21-47). Two of these examples deal with anger and revenge. Jesus' statement about anger is instructive, but first it is alarming and disturbing. On reading the Scripture, "But I say to you that every one who is angry with his brother shall be liable to judgment; whoever insults his brother shall be liable to the council, and whoever says, 'You fool!' shall be liable to the hell of fire" (Matt. 5:22), one gets the impression that anger is just as bad as murder. But I certainly would rather have someone be angry at me than to murder me.

What is Jesus saying in the Sermon on the Mount? Jesus Himself got angry. Was He guilty of murder? The word translated "is angry" (Matt. 5:22) is a present participle conveying continuous action. *The New English Bible* reads, "Anyone who nurses anger . . . must be brought to judgement." That captures the intent of the Greek language. Jesus was forever addressing Himself to the motives for people's actions. He was concerned about how the process began. He knew there was an intricate correlation between roots and fruits in people's lives. Jesus' words regarding anger expressed a radical protest toward people who allow their anger to fester and eventually poison the relationship with another human being. What Jesus said was that if people nursed their anger, they fed it, causing it to grow larger.

Nursing anger sends a message to the body that it is in great danger and needs stronger, quicker reactions and responses in order to survive. To continue to feed anger will result in being devoured by it. To nurse anger is to be sucked dry. Frederick Buechner described nursing anger when he wrote:

> Of the Seven Deadly Sins, anger is possibly the most fun. To lick your wounds, to smack your lips over grievances long past, to roll over your tongue the prospect of bitter confrontations still to come, to savor to the last toothsome morsel both the pain you are given and the pain you are giving back—in many ways it is a feast fit for a king. The chief drawback is that what you are wolfing down is yourself. The skeleton at the feast is you.[2]

The first step in dealing creatively and healthily with our anger is to recognize it and call it by name. A very significant event is recorded in Genesis 2 when Adam was invited to name the animals. The Bible treats a name with significance. To name something is to acknowledge its existence. Naming anger is the beginning point for being responsible for action motivated by anger and for being in control of anger. Unrecognized anger goes unnoticed and unnamed. It becomes demonic because it gives birth to hatred rather than to nurturing love. To ignore anger is to abdicate control over it. The result is: we collaborate with sin and make ourselves vulnerable to the demonic.[3] Thomas Aquinas said, "He who is angry or afraid is not praised or blamed, but only he who while in this state behaves either properly or not."[4]

To nurse anger is to behave improperly because nursing anger is to insult the one with whom I am angry. To harbor anger and keep it alive tears away respect and appreciation for other people. Do we not often consider friends, business associates, and fellow church members as brothers and sisters, but spouses and children as people on a lower level of value and importance than brothers and sisters? Peggy, my wife, brought this point home to me one day when I was venting my anger by asking, "Why don't you treat us with the same consideration that you do people at church?"

One of our difficulties in dealing constructively with our anger is our desire to cling to a few little hurts or one or two big ones and to stockpile them in our arsenals. Then, when the next disagreement comes, we can go to the well of our resentments and hurt feelings and draw enough ammunition to blow away the person with whom we are angry. The result is a Pyrrhic victory. When Pyrrhus, the king of Epirus, led the Grecian forces into southern Italy in 281 BC, his twenty-five-thousand men, remarkably well equipped with cavalry and elephants, met and defeated the Roman forces. His losses, however, were so great that Pyrrhus was compelled to utter his celebrated lament, "Another such victory over the Romans and we are undone."[5] So it is with our relationships when we nurse our anger. We insult our brothers and sisters and call them fools. Another victory like that, and both they and we will be ruined.

Nursing anger leads to resentment. Resentment means to feel again, and thus involves revisiting and reliving an old conflict. Resentment is an attitude in which a person refuses reconciliation. Frederick Nietzche is credited with saying that nothing on earth consumes a person like resentment.

Several years ago, a convict rehabilitation program developed seven steps that were essential for one who had been imprisoned to reenter society and not be a repeat offender. People who followed this approach were known as the Seven Steppers. The fifth step in their litany of commitment is: "Deciding that our freedom is worth more than our resentments, we are using that power to help free ourselves from these resentments."

Was not this the approach Jesus suggested toward worship? When a person brought his offering and remembered someone had something against him, he was to seek reconciliation before giving his offering. Isn't this a strange sequence of action? We would expect that if someone had something against us, he ought to come to *us.* That is the way we live, isn't it? Our litany of "wreckonciliation" says, "I'm not having another thing to do with her until she says she's sorry. I did nothing wrong. It's not my responsibility to straighten out this relationship."

But why are we who have been wronged expected to take the initiative for reconciliation? When we have been wronged, even through absolutely no fault of our own, the wrong done to us is a threat to our personhood, and our natural response is anger because a breach has occurred in the relationship. If we are to have close encounters of the right kind, as soon as we recognize that someone has something against us, we need to initiate reconciliation. Our model for this is God our Redeemer who feels the break in relationship with us and who seeks us. We have sinned against God, but who is it that initiates restoring the relationship? The God in the Bible is forever seeking to restore relationships with people who have committed wrongs.

What does the altar have to do with this? What is the altar? Where is it? The altar is a religious symbol. It represents the presence of God and is the focal point of one's relationship with God. The altar may be a solitary place or a place of public worship. The altar introduces God into the situation, so no longer can I react and respond on the basis of just how I feel or what I want. The altar also is a safe haven where it is OK for things to surface that I have submerged into my unconsciousness. For me, anger that is not brought to the altar results in a tremendous energy drain. Having not been named and dealt with, the anger runs rampant, unchecked through life. Bringing anger to the altar is a means of inviting God's help in dealing with anger. When we are angry, sin is couching at the door.

Simmer Down Before Sundown

For centuries, anger and sin have been equated in Christianity. In the Middle Ages anger was identified as one of the seven deadly sins. Anger has gotten either bad press or no press from the church. Nevertheless, in biblical material godly people are described as those who dealt constructively with their anger rather than being people who never got angry (Prov. 14:17; 14:29; 16:32; 19:11; Ps. 4:4). These passages deal with people who were careful with their anger rather than idolize people who never got angry.

I recall the relief and release I experienced the day I stumbled upon the words of Paul, "Be angry but do not sin; do not let the sun go down on your anger, and give no opportunity to the devil" (Eph. 4:26-27). For a long time I paid attention only to the first part of verse 26. I had heard a lot of commands from the church: go, teach, preach, baptize, do this, don't do that, but never had I heard anyone say, "Be angry." When and where I grew up, anger was taught by inference to be a sin. Adults in my childhood frowned disapproval on anyone who expressed anger verbally or physically, although no consideration was given to what a person's countenance might be communicating. There were occasions of verbal abuse when anger got dressed up and found a place to explode, but when the dust settled no one mentioned either the angry outburst or what caused the anger. The message I internalized was, "Don't get angry because anger is wrong. Nice people don't get angry. Christians are nice people." Because I considered myself a Christian, whenever I got angry I told myself I wasn't angry. You may have had a similar reaction or felt tremendous guilt for feeling angry. That is double trouble.

What a shocking relief it was to read in the Bible the dual command to be angry but not to sin. I went aside at this burning bush because this was holy ground for me, a place where I could learn more about God and about me. It was sometime later that I began to struggle with the next phrase of Paul, which said to simmer down before sundown. I didn't have too much trouble doing that when I got angry just after sunrise, but on those days when I got angry at 5:00 PM I had to work triple time to simmer down before sundown. Most days I didn't make it. The question I continued to raise was: How could I do what Paul was recommending?

What about the distance I experience in a relationship where I have had a major role in causing the alienation? Forgiveness is essential and yet very difficult for me. I wonder how many times I have been wrong in my relationships with others. How many times have I admitted my mistakes and sought forgiveness? This is where life gets tough for me. Three small words: "I was wrong," three more small words: "I am sorry," two more words: "Forgive me." Eight words—so few, so powerful—but they are so difficult for too many of us to say with integrity: "I was wrong; I am sorry; forgive me." People are never stronger than when they admit their failures, wrongs, and weaknesses.

In our intimate relationships, we experience the most anger and have the greatest opportunity to learn how to cope with our anger in constructive ways. Marriage and family living generate more anger than other social situations. Abuse, verbal or physical or both, results from the misuse of anger. Murder is an extreme form of abuse whose roots are buried in anger or buried anger. The majority of murders are committed by people who know their victims, usually family members of close friends. One suggestion to achieve longevity is to have no friends and to have nothing to do with family members. However, these actions are contrary to our nature and need and contrary to Jesus' suggestions about responding to anger. The inner failure of a close relationship usually occurs because the persons involved have been unable to achieve mutual love and intimacy. "The failure to achieve love and intimacy is almost always due to the inability of the persons concerned to deal creatively with anger."[6]

Anger is an indicator of danger that we feel, and is part of the early-warning system when something is threatening our well-being. Physiological changes occur in our bodies when we are angry. Our heart rates increase, breathing speeds up, muscles tense, adrenalin pours into the bloodstream, and anticoagulants in the blood diminish. There is an immediate surge of energy as our bodies prepare to fight or to take flight in response to a threat. There also is an increase in mental awareness. Anger is an emotional response to a stimulus and is part of our human survival kit.

Some threats, such as nearly having an automobile accident, are common to all of us. After the fright has subsided, the anger surges at whoever nearly caused us to wreck. In some circumstances, however, what is a threat to one may not be to another. The week I began writing this material my family went bowling. When I reached for my wallet to pay for my bowling shoes, it was not there. Someone had picked my pocket! I was angry at somebody. Then I remembered I had left my wallet at home. Only a fool would be so unprepared! I was angry at myself. I would leave my family and rush home to get the wallet. The quicker I could get my wallet, the less chance there was for me to be embarrassed for being unprepared. Then it was discovered that my daughter had money with her, and the family persuaded me to stay and bowl. We had an enjoyable time, but I had to process my anger and deal with it. This incident was a threat to my view of myself, and anger was my emotional response to the threat.

The value of anger is its impelling force toward action, but how can the action be positive and build up a relationship rather than tear it down? The two most common ways of dealing with anger are suppression and ventilation. Suppression is probably our immediate first step when we get angry. It is a process by which anger is buried alive. The anger festers and poisons, eventually working its way out of a person in damaging and bizarre ways. Suppressed anger erupts as sarcasm, withdrawal, silence, or nagging. Suppressed anger at a spouse may surface as demanding or refusing sexual intercourse, flirtation, or involvement in an extramarital affair. Suppression of anger often involves refusing to admit that one feels angry. This is dishonest, untruthful, and a distortion of reality.

When was the most recent time you sensed someone was angry with you, and you asked, "What's wrong?" The response was, "Nothing." When did you last give such a response rather than identify and admit your anger? Such a response is a double message. The word conveys one message, but the tone conveys an opposite one. The person denying the anger is being untruthful. Ulcers, high blood pressure, and some heart problems are physical results of suppressing anger. Depression and suicide are two forms of emotional sickness caused by the suppression of anger.

To suppress anger is to swallow it. There is a limit to the amount of anger people can swallow before they get sick. Some will eat excessively to help them swallow their anger. An extremely overweight adolescent girl was referred to a pastoral counselor because her family relationships were frayed with tension. Her counselor sensed early that in some way her obesity was related to her anger although she denied ever getting angry. During one session the girl reported an incident with her mother. Her body language clearly communicated anger. The counselor asked her what she did in response to the incident. She said she made a double recipe of brownies and ate all of them herself. Further discussion revealed this to be a regular practice for her. Food, especially something sweet, helped her swallow her anger. Damaging our bodies physically or emotionally because of mishandled anger is sinful.

Ventilation is the other common way we deal with anger. Venting anger often is akin to the eruption of Mount Saint Helen's. We do not discriminate about who gets burned by our heat. All we know is that we just have to let it out. We cannot hold our anger any longer. This willingness to vent anger is healthier than suppressing it for the one who is angry, but venting anger usually is destructive to any relationship. Often anger that is vented is like mail delivered to the wrong address. Vented anger usually is misdirected.

A cartoon portrayed this well. A man who had had a rough day at work arrived home exasperated. As soon as his wife said hello, he growled and shouted at her. She turned and yelled at the oldest child who screamed at her sister who yelled at her brother who kicked the dog. The caption read, "It would have been better if the man had kicked the dog." Vented anger often is projected onto an innocent person who catches the brunt of anger that is misdirected. Vented anger is an overreaction. Ventilation usually follows some suppression of anger which means that more anger is ventilated than was caused by the current incident. Damaging others emotionally or physically by venting our anger is sinful.

It is impossible to avoid getting angry. People use a variety of terms to identify their anger. They say they are hurt, disappointed, miffed, upset, disturbed, irritated, frustrated, suffering righteous indignation, mad, or angry. Neither suppressing nor venting anger proves to be a constructive method of coping with anger. What Jesus suggested about reconciliation (Matt. 5:21-26) is what David Mace has identified as processing anger.[7] Mace applied his suggestions to marriage. His suggestions are workable in any intimate relationship. If we are unable to process our anger in our intimate relationships, we will not cope with anger very well in the larger family of human beings. In Jesus' view of life, we are all siblings of one another and children of one parent: God.

The first step in processing anger is to give each other the right to be angry with the other without judgements or penalties. Anger is a healthy emotion, and no one has the power to prevent anger. In order to process anger, however, it is necessary to identify it and communicate to the one with whom you are angry that you are angry. It is helpful to remember that no one makes you angry. Your anger is a response to a stimulus that threatens you. Why can it not be as acceptable to say, "I'm feeling angry," as it is to say, "I'm feeling hungry"? If we would deal with our anger as often as we deal with our hunger, we probably could simmer down before sundown.

There is a distinction between acknowledging anger and venting anger. This distinction leads to a second step in processing anger, which is a commitment by both parties not to attack each other. This involves a covenant by both parties that is based on their concern that the relationship win rather than one of them. If the relationship does not win, then both parties lose, whether the parties are spouses, fellow church members, or next-door neighbors. The result is that compassionate concern begins to develop for each other. What would happen in your relationships if you committed yourself never to attack anyone? If this pattern were followed in marriages, families, and close friendships, then greater understanding of how and why the state of anger arises would develop, and the ability to communicate this would be easier and clearer.

Even when the right to be angry has been granted and distinction has been made between acknowledging and venting anger, the anger is still present and will not be processed until the stimulus is recognized and removed. This is the third step. Jesus said the one who realizes that another is holding something against her is to take the initiative. Accept the fact that a state of anger evoked by another is an integral part of a relationship and that both have an equal responsibility to clear it up. Anger is a barrier between people which must be removed by both parties acting together. Unless this is done the relationship will be damaged, and if the anger is allowed to continue, the damage will be progressive. Jesus said that when anger is nursed it leads to insults, insults lead to labeling, name-calling, and hatred. To call a person a fool is to declare her out of the realm of help. Only God can make that decision, although in incidents like this we often attempt to be God.

On another occasion Jesus gave similar instructions concerning the initiative of reconciliation (Matt. 18:15-17). The instruction is that if someone sins against you, go to that one and seek reconciliation. If the guilty one is unreceptive, then take one or two people with you. If the one who did you wrong remains unreceptive, then bring the situation to the church. If reconciliation still does not occur, let the relationship end. If anger is nursed, the relationship cannot be nurtured. The purpose of Jesus' instruction about anger is to process anger so the relationship can be nurtured. This approach enables us to deal with anger as it arises, which is essential if we are to simmer down before sundown.

The Cheek-Turning Principle

Thomas Jefferson approached the Bible with scissors in one hand and paste in the other, cutting out what he did not like and piecing together what was left. Although few of us would go to the Jeffersonian extreme, we do have our own condensed versions of the Bible. We "cut out" sections by avoiding them.

One section that is left out of the Bible of too many people is the instruction Jesus gave about revenge. Jesus took the law of retaliation to a degree of implication that it had never been taken previously. The rule of an eye for an eye had been introduced to restrain greater evil. Early in the human enterprise, unlimited retaliation was the way people dealt with wrong done to them. Actually, the eye for an eye rule was movement toward limited retaliation. In the movie about his life, Gandhi said that if we lived by this rule, all of us would be walking around blind and toothless. As civilization expanded, people discovered the positive value of loving their neighbors as a means of improving community life. Along came Jesus urging people not to resist evil and to love their enemies. This rule of unlimited love met great resistance then, and we resist its application in our lives today.

Our resistance is not because of ignorance. We understand very well the instruction from Jesus that we turn the other cheek, but we do not dare practice such a principle. We cloak our resistance in an interpretation that a college classmate gave to this instruction, "The Bible says to turn the other cheek, but it doesn't say what to do after that."

The calling of Christ invites us to rise above our culture, which is very difficult to do. "You have to defend yourself." "You can't let people walk over you." "Fight fire with fire." "The best defense is a strong offense." "We need to be strong in order to deter attack from others." Ad infinitum go the statements and suggestions of what is practical about opposition and aggression. We dismiss Jesus' cheek-turning principle as too idealistic. A statement attributed to G. K. Chesterton says that Christianity has not been tried and found wanting, but it has been found difficult and not tried.

Jesus said, "Do not resist evil with evil" (Matt. 5:39, AP). The Greek allows for this reading as well as the Revised Standard Version translation which reads, "Do not resist one who is evil." Jesus certainly resisted one who was evil in His wilderness temptation experiences and with His statement to Peter, "Get behind Me, Satan!" However, Jesus never resisted anyone with evil.

To resist with evil results in more evil. This was illustrated vividly in Washington, DC, on November 27, 1982. A Klu Klux Klan rally was held, causing hatred to breed more hatred. The Klan, by its existence and presence, says that its members hate blacks. Many blacks respond with hatred. During the rally, there were many who demonstrated peacefully against the Klan in a constructive resistance to the evil of racial prejudice. Many of those who demonstrated against the Klan felt hated and hated those who hated them. Then they vented their hatred onto the police who were protecting the Klan members. This was a destructive way to resist evil. The ensuing riot was a frightening illustration of what results when evil is resisted with evil.

An event that happened during my adolescent years has helped teach me the value of resisting evil, but not *with* evil. I was fifteen at the time, and my mother and I were in an angry argument, the issue I cannot remember. Whatever the issue, she felt I needed physical punishment. She attempted to slap me, and I blocked her hand as a reflex action. Her anger increased. The same series of actions were repeated after which she was infuriated and insisted that she slap me. With all the self-control I could call on, I stood facing her and allowed her to slap me, then I saw power and control drain from her face. As I later reflected on this event, I discovered that day to have been the beginning of the decline of Mother's power and control over me. It also signified the day that I began to take more responsibility for my personhood and my actions. I suspect that was a frightening day for her because it signaled a significant change in our relationship. At least on this one occasion my resistance of my mother was not with evil.

A further application of the cheek-turning principle is Jesus' instruction that we are to love our enemies. Here He stretches the law again to be inclusive and suggests that loving our enemies is essential if we are to be complete and whole as God is whole. To love only those who love us is no accomplishment. People in every religion and in no religion do that. As children of God, Jesus challenges us to model our life-styles after the living God.

Probably the language Jesus spoke was Aramaic. He could not have said *perfect* in Aramaic. He would have said either *shalom* or *tamin* which conveys the sense of completion or wholeness.[8] In the Greek language the word *teleios* identifies something as perfect beyond which there is not further advance in excellence or quality. This word is not used to describe ethical behavior but is purely formal as in describing one who has reached the limit of professional ability.[9] In this passage the analogy is that as God is unrestricted in His goodness, thus the disciples of Jesus are to be total in their love, including their enemies in their broad sweep of love. The word used in Matthew (5:48) has the same root as does the verb translated in John's Gospel when Jesus said, "It is finished," (John 19:30) as His life ended.

When we make the statement "You must be perfect" to mean that we have to be morally perfect for God to love us, we immediately begin repressing our dark sides, our sins, wounds, and fantasies. Our enemies are not only or always people outside ourselves. Often our enemies are identified as people beyond ourselves, but close examination reveals how similar they are to us. Our enmity with them is that we see our dark sides in them. Just as this happens on an individual and personal basis, enmity is multiplied in intensity between groups of people who accentuate their differences. The intensity is increased manyfold by nations that emphasize the differences in their ideologies from other nations. Is this not much of the fuel that fires the feud between the United States and the Soviet Union? Do we not in many ways represent each other's dark sides? If we make Jesus' words mean ethical and moral perfection, we make it impossible to love our enemies because we can't love those upon whom we unconsciously are dumping our self-hatred.

Jesus' instruction about the cheek-turning principle and loving our enemies was not just a pipe dream. It was a principle by which He lived and because of which He died. Ironically, it was the religious establishment that did Jesus in. This Galilean strolled through Palestine drawing ever-enlarging circles by loving His enemies, turning first one cheek and then the other, and it cost Him His life. The crunch for us is that there are many things for which we will live: our families, our jobs, a better life, and success. There is not much, if anything, for which we will die and certainly not in some inglorious situation where we would turn the other cheek. Someone might call us cowardly, crazy, or both. We really wish Jesus had never said anything about turning the other cheek or loving our enemies because these statements indict us. Yet, when it comes to responding to anger, the cheek-turning principle has redeeming value.

Summary

Jesus warned us about nursing our anger. The Bible has numerous illustrations of the destructiveness it causes. The Cain-and-Abel story is the oldest. Paul integrated the teaching of Jesus with his wisdom to the Ephesians to "simmer down before sundown." The cheek-turning principle illustrates the value of resisting evil but not *with* evil. Jesus' instructions about constructive uses of anger and loving our enemies are established on the premise that every person is worth redeeming. God's love is perfect—totally complete in that it includes everyone. We are to be as complete in our love of all creation as God is. We need to start by naming and admitting our anger and finding ways to process it rather than either suppressing or venting it. Then we will be responding to anger redemptively which is essential if there is to be reconciliation.

Notes

1. Kenneth E. Moyer, *The Physiology of Hostility* (Chicago: Markham Press, 1971), p. 23.

2. Frederick Buechner, *Wishful Thinking: A Theological ABC* (San Francisco: Harper and Row, 1973), p. 2.

3. Andrew D. Lester, *Coping with Your Anger: A Christian Guide* (Philadelphia: The Westminster Press, 1983), p. 54.

4. Quoted by Samuel Southard, *Anger in Love* (Philadelphia: The Westminster Press, 1973), p. 15.

5. Emily Morrison Beck, ed. *Bartlett's Familiar Quotations* (Boston: Little, Brown and Co., 1980), p. 92.

6. David Mace, "Love, Anger, and Intimacy," *Proceedings of the 1979 Christian Life Commission Seminar on Help for Families* (Nashville: Broadman Press).

7. David Mace, *Love and Anger in Marriage* (Grand Rapids, Mich.: The Zondervan Corporation, 1982), p. 79.

8. Walter Wink, *Transforming Bible Study* (Nashville: Abingdon Press, 1980), p. 51.

9. Gerhard Dellin, "Teleios," *Theological Dictionary of the New Testament* (Grand Rapids, Mich.: William B. Eerdmans Publishing Company, 1964), vol. 8, p. 68.

2
Responding to Hypocrisy

Mathew 23: 13-36

The Pharisees were the religious leaders with whom Jesus had the most in common, with whom He had the most conflict, and apparently were the ones with whom He got angriest most often. His anger with them occasionally was expressed nonverbally, "And he looked around at them with anger, grieved at their hardness of heart" (Mark 3:5). He also verbalized His anger with them, "You are like whitewashed tombs, which outwardly appear beautiful, but within they are full of dead men's bones and all uncleanness" (Matt. 23:27).

Jesus' confrontation with the Pharisees often seemed to revolve around some form of hypocrisy. The value of anger is its impelling force toward action. With regard to hypocrisy, Jesus' anger motivated Him to respond redemptively to those who were hypocritical.

The Gift of Discernment

Jesus was forever seeking to get at the motive for an action rather than to deal with the results. He preferred to prevent a problem than to cure all of the disease caused after the problem had exploded. His efforts at cutting through hypocrisy are contained in His instructions about judging (Matt. 7:1-12). Included in these verses is one of the most difficult statements in the Bible. "Judge not, that you be not judged. For with the judgment you pronounce you will be judged, and the measure you give will be the measure you get." (Matt. 7:1-2). Judgment is the dominant theme throughout the seventh chapter of Matthew. Obviously, Jesus is making judgments about people and encouraging His disciples to do the same when He said to be on guard against false prophets (v. 15). Forming judgments seems to be an inescapable function of the mind. Was Jesus suggesting that we train our minds not to function? Too many of us already function with untrained minds.

To judge anything is to evaluate it on the basis of criteria. In many instances the criteria are well thought out and known in advance. Judges at county fairs evaluate homemade jelly on the basis of appearance, taste, and texture. A courtroom judge makes a decision on a property settlement case after examining evidence from both sides. We make judgments about people every day. "She is attractive." "He is pleasant." "They hate each other." These statements clearly express judgments and indicate that our criteria are based primarily on personal preference.

The term *judgment* began as a legal term, but centuries ago it began to be used as a theological term. That was problematic then, and it continues to be confusing. Most often in religious life, judgment has a negative connotation, a dooming mood, and a means of striking fear in the lives of people. I want to examine here the ambivalence that Jesus seemed to have about judgment and then draw from Him some criteria to assist us in developing the gift of discernment.

Jesus' Ambivalence

The author of John's Gospel detected Jesus' ambivalence about judgment. He recorded that God did not send His Son into the world to judge the world but to save it (3:17). Jesus said about those who listened to Him, "If anyone hears my sayings and does not keep them, I do not judge him; for I did not come to judge the world but to save the world" (12:47). One another occasion, Jesus responded to what seemed to be superficial decisions, "You judge according to the flesh, I judge no one" (8:15).

The writer of John also recorded Jesus saying, "For judgment I came into the world" (9:39). In another place, John quoted Jesus, "The Father judges no one, but has given all judgment to the Son,

. . . and has give him authority to execute judgment, because he is the Son of man" (5:22-27).

Luke recorded a dialogue of Jesus with a man and parable of Jesus that may shed some light on Jesus' meaning about judgment. A man came to Jesus with a request. "Teacher, bid my brother divide the inheritance with me," and Jesus replied, "Man, who made me a judge or divider over you?" (Luke 12:13). This was a strong rebuff to one who was seeking Jesus' help. Why did Jesus respond so strongly? Could it be that Jesus knew in this situation that judgment meant division? Division over money already existed between the brothers, and Jesus knew it was impossible to heal division with division.

One of the strangest and most puzzling of Jesus' parables is recorded in the sixteenth chapter of Luke. Commonly it is referred to as the parable of the unjust or dishonest steward. This man had mismanaged the property of his boss and wasted his boss's money. His boss became suspicious and asked that the manager give an account of his work. The manager knew he was going to lose his job. He was in a quandary about what to do. Here is another illustration that necessity is the mother of invention. Under the pressure and duress of impending unemployment, the manager devised a scheme which he hoped would benefit him after the firing. He went to the people who owed money to his boss, loans he had made in behalf of his boss, and called them in at discount prices. He did more than reduce the percentage of interest; he even reduced the principal. He told one borrower his debt could be cut in half by paying the debt immediately. He promised another man a 20 percent discount for immediate payment. Thus the manager had at least two people indebted to him when he was out of work. The surprise of the story is the boss who lost money on the deal appreciated the ingenuity of the manager. Apparently, Jesus told this story to illustrate that the manager found a way to promote reunion. Even this scoundrel sought to overcome division with reconciliation and reunion.

The word translated *judge* in Matthew (7:1) is translated *condemn* in John (3:17). Perhaps this distinction can be helpful to us. To condemn people is to declare them beyond recovery. Surely this is the intent of Jesus when He told His disciples, "Condemn not, so that you will not be condemned. For with the condemnation you pronounce, you will be condemned, and the measure you give will be the measure you receive" (Matt. 7:2, author's paraphrase).

Is not Jesus inviting us to follow His practice in this matter? Surely He was not suggesting that people close their eyes to all distinctions between good and evil. That would be impossible. Jesus was forbidding us to condemn (judge) as if condemnation were the last word, the decisive thing, the key to the realization of God's purpose with us. Then Jesus used a very humorous hyperbole to illustrate the foolishness of our condemnation. Humor is a helpful way to communicate anger provided the humor is not used to disguise, deny, or misdirect the anger.

Jesus pointed out how quickly we become ophthalmologists, suddenly seeing splinters in everybody's eyes. We begin immediately to perform surgery on others' eyes, failing to realize that the splinters we see so clearly in others are the reflections of the planks that are in our eyes. How often the contempt and condemnation we hold for others is a projection of our own guilt! Jesus said it is a boomerang. The judgment and condemnation we receive is in proportion and degree to that which we have given. This understanding helps clear up Jesus' ambivalence about judgment and provides a basis for criteria for discernment.

Criteria for Discernment

Jesus certainly evaluated His disciples as well as the Pharisees. He judged the Pharisees in a way that has tended to make their name a reproach forever. Jesus seemed to acknowledge that people are going to evaluate each other. Was He not saying, "Be careful how you assess another's character, for in so doing you unconsciously assess yourself and give yourself away?" Jesus offered some criteria by which we may develop the gift of discernment.

First, there are to be no double standards. The standard of conduct is to be the same for others and for oneself. There are many double standards which we have supported in our culture. Many families have made allowances in conduct based on the gender of the child. Institutions have done the same. During my college days, the women students had curfew, but the men did not. Many employers have unequal pay scales. Women doing the same job as men often have received less pay. In the church, many aspects of ministry have been off limits to women. In the Southern Baptist Convention, the Woman's Missionary Union is an auxiliary of the Convention rather than an agency of it. In the early years when the WMU made a report to the Convention, a man gave the report because women were not permitted to speak to the group.

I would not be surprised to learn that you hold a double standard of conduct with regard to yourself and your pastor, expecting the ethical and moral conduct of your pastor to be better than yours although you and your pastor claim to be disciples of the same Lord. All are to be measured by the same moral and ethical yardstick.

A second criterion for developing the gift of discernment is self-examination. A woman who was caught in adultery was brought to Jesus. Apparently, the man was caught also. Why was he not brought to Jesus? Why was the man exempt from stoning? The Pharisees asked Jesus what should be done. After doodling in the sand, Jesus said that whoever was without sin should throw the first stone. Jesus wrote in the sand again, and when He looked up, only He and the woman remained. He asked, "Does no one judge (condemn) you?" She said, "No one." Jesus replied, "I don't either. Go and sin no more" (John 8:7, author). Based on our claims about Jesus being sinless and by the standard Jesus proposed, we would insist that Jesus had the right to do the stoning, but He did not. To have done so would have snuffed out any hope of recovery for the woman.

Certainly the splinter-log hyperbole recorded by Matthew illustrates clearly that self-examination is essential if we are to develop the gift of discernment. The sin of another in comparison to ours is that of splinter to log, but we want to reverse the ratio and call attention to how much worse others are than we. We are not to ignore the splinter in another's eye. It is our business to assist others in freeing them from splinters that impair their vision. We are in a much better condition for this ministry, however, after the two-by-fours have been removed from our eyes.

A third criterion in developing discernment is to be cautious when handling priceless lives. Every life is priceless. Jesus's way of stating this was, "Relate to other people like you want them to relate to you" (Matt. 7:12, author). Too often our approach is to do to others *before* they can do to us, *so* they cannot do to us, or *because* they did to us. Jesus could have urged His followers to develop a policy of uninvolvement, encouraging them, "Don't do anything to hurt anybody." This is a negative stance of withdrawal. Jesus demonstrated a positive, active involvement calling on His disciples to demonstrate in their relationships how they wanted to be treated. We need to show one another love, not just tell about it. When we view judgment—condemnation—as the last word, we become careless with what is costly: priceless human life.

One man has given some sound advice to which we are to adhere before we utter a judgment. We need to ask three questions: (1) Is it true? (2) Is it necessary? (3) Is it kind? These questions help us temper any judgment with mercy which aids us in being cautious when we handle priceless lives. We may make some assumptions that a person is getting what he deserves, or he can handle whatever we dish out. We may function on the old adage, "If you can't stand the heat, get out of the kitchen." Probably what we don't know is how much heat the person endured before we began stoking the fire. We are dealing with priceless lives, and we need to be cautious.

Very often when we use the phrase "Judge not," we mean, "Judge *me* not." We have not real objection about judging others. Actually, we are usually glad to lend our voices in announcing the judgments on others, especially if by doing so we can gain some converts to our views or elevate our status.

Our tendency is for judgment to be the final word. It is difficult for us to change our opinions once we have made a decision, whether positive or negative. It is an inescapable psychological fact that every person we meet makes an impression on us. If the meeting is lengthy or repeated, or a relationship develops into a continuing association, then the initial impression hardens into a judgment that influences the course of the relationship.

Our impulse is to judge in the sense of condemning others, with our judgement being the final word. On the one hand, if we refrain from condemning someone who has been wrong according to our standards, we conclude that judgment won't be done, and the person will get away with the wrong she committed. On the other hand, we desire to be judged favorably by others because their lack of approval and esteem is hard to bear.

We are challenged to develop the gift of discernment, so we will not throw away or destroy that which is holy and priceless. The gift of discernment will keep us from acting as judges who condemn others beyond hope or help. The gift of discernment requires that we use the same standard for others that we use for ourselves. Self-examination is essential before we dare move to encourage another to make changes in his life. We have no way of knowing all the facts.

Often the more we know a person and her struggles, the more difficult it is to condemn her. Condemnation only widens the gulf rather than bridging the gap. What if Jesus had begun with Zacchaeus by accusing him of overcharging people on their taxes? Or what if He had attacked the woman's character who washed His feet with her tears? Jesus permitted and facilitated the process for people to evaluate themselves. Jesus' dealings with people were toward reconciliation and reunion so that any confrontation He had with people was intended as a move toward bridge building between them and Him. His responses to people were redemptive. This is the purpose of the gift of discernment, to build bridges so people can return from the islands of exile where they have been banished by others, so they can climb down out of the sycamore trees where they have fled.

Pharisees

It was the Pharisees' lack of the gift of discernment that concerned Jesus. He perceived their condemnation was causing people to flee from the Temple rather than to be drawn to it. People were feeling hopeless and helpless, and these despairing feelings were being fueled by the Pharisees' double standards.

Jesus was closer in His thinking and teaching to the Pharisees than to any other group in Judaism, yet some of His harshest, angriest words were spoken to them. Perhaps it was His affinity to the Pharisees that enabled Jesus to be so perceptive about their life-styles and religious practices. A brief examination of the Pharisees will be helpful in our examination of the anger that Jesus felt toward them and His constructive use of anger to respond redemptively to the hypocritical Pharisees.

The strength and significance of the Pharisees reached their apex between 135-105 BC. During this period they emerged as a strongly established and powerful religious-political party in the Jewish theocratic state. The term *pharisee* means "one who is separate." The Pharisees were the result of a lay involvement within Judaism that grew out of a revival of the unresolved conflict between the roles of the prophet and the priest in Israel.

Israel had become a united people under David, and during Solomon's reign the Temple became the focal point of unity and identity. When the Temple was destroyed and many of the leaders were deported in 587 BC, Israel's identity struggle was reopened and reexamined. If you have ever had a fire destroy your home or business, you know the devastation it caused. Have you ever been a member of a congregation whose building was renovated completely or destroyed? Do you recall the attachment you had to that building and the struggle you had adjusting to the new or renewed structure? The Israelites experienced a devastating loss in 587 BC. In order to retain their identity, they shifted the focal point of their identity from the Temple to the Law, the essence of which was the Ten Commandments.

The Pharisees were those men who in their meticulous observance of the Law separated themselves from uncleanliness, including the people of the land who were considered unclean. Uncleanliness was treated as a contagious disease. During the Exile, the Ten Commandments became the rallying point of identity for Judaism, and the Pharisees accepted the task of interpreting, applying, and illustrating the Ten Commandments which were defined by more than six-hundred rules. The Pharisees were interested in the progress and development of Judaism in the worship and service of God. They were the liberals and progressives in the Jewish society for the two centuries preceding the life of Jesus.

Eventually, the Israelites were permitted to return to Jerusalem and rebuild the Temple. Of course, not all the Jews returned to Israel, and the Temple never quite regained the centrality it had held in the pre-Exilic period. First the prophet Ezekiel, and then others, pointed out that God was not limited to a geographical boundary. This awareness intensified the focus of the Law.

A great deal of political turmoil tore through Israel, especially as the Roman Empire flexed its muscles and expanded its domination. Eventually, Israel was occupied by Roman forces, and the Pharisees separated themselves from the political scene as long as religious life was unaffected. They sold their political allegiance to Rome for a bowl of religious protection. As a religious group, the Pharisees had no political ambitions and were content with any government that allowed them to carry out ceremonial law. They accepted the Scriptures (Old Testament) and detailed regulations and rules of oral and ceremonial law as their instructions for living. They believed in fate— a person's life was planned and ordered by God.[1] They believed in and hoped for the coming of the Messiah, and they believed in angels, spirits, and in the resurrection of the dead.

The Pharisees sensed that their influence had waned gradually over the years. They became entrenched in the need to preserve rules and regulations as they lost power and felt their security threatened. Rule keeping became increasingly valuable and by Jesus' time had become more important than people. Jesus observed that whenever religious rules and the needs of the people were in conflict, the Pharisees considered the rules more important than the people. By the beginning of the first century AD, Pharisaism had become a sterile religion of codified tradition, regulating every part of life by rules, stringently requiring separation. Consequently, the Pharisees became legalists.

Legalists in religion seek to achieve a standard that they conclude God will accept, usually expressed in some form of outward performances that can be demonstrated, measured, and advertised. Legalists perceive God accepting people on the basis of what they do. Conformity to the rules becomes paramount for acceptance by God.

During unsettling times, people will grasp for a kind of security that is as tangible as Linus's blanket and often just as useless. Usually these people either don't recognize this need or are too scared to admit it. Usually there are those in religious circles who portray life in distinct black-and-white terms offering simplistic solutions to the complexities of life. Who is there among us who at times does not wish for an easy answer to all of life's questions? This desire was verbalized in the movie *Silkwood* when the leading man said, "Just give me problems I can solve." That is what the Pharisees seemed to want, and they continually reduced life into manageable rules they could obey. The Pharisees were concerned with external evidences of their cleanliness, which meant both obeying the rules and excluding those who didn't.

Periodically, some of the children in my neighborhood form a club. Usually they publish a list, either oral or written, of the club members. Also published are the rules that determine who is included and who is excluded as club members. The result is the construction of an emotional, invisible wall. Those who are in make decisions about those who are out. Anger rises as exclusiveness increases. Fortunately, in many neighborhoods this is a game that children play briefly. Unfortunately, too many adults play the same games in religion and make religion into a club, one to join by abiding by the rules.

When this is the approach, religion becomes a restrictive set of rules to be kept rather than an expansive faith to be shared. The movie, *Oh*

God had an insightful line when Jim Landers said to God, "I thought religion was your business." God responded, "'Religion is easy, but I'm asking you to have faith." Religion is easy when (1) it is defined as rule keeping, (2) the rules are simple, (3) one knows what the rules are, and (4) one finds acceptance through conformity.

Religion thus defined, however, results in rules being more important than people. Those who do not conform to the rules are excluded, and a regimented approach to life develops. Joy, humor, and laughter are lost. Voltaire's insight is perceptive: "God is a comedian playing to an audience that is afraid to laugh." Up go the walls that separate people. Some are walled in while others are walled out.

This was the approach of the Pharisees during Jesus' lifetime. I have offered this brief sketch of the development of Pharisaism because this is the terrain in which Jesus lived out His life. Understanding Pharisaism has been helpful to me in perceiving more clearly and comprehending more readily the angry responses Jesus made to the Pharisees. We in the contemporary church are the new Pharisees.

Confronting Hypocrisy

I often have heard it said that the church is full of hypocrites. Nearly as often I have refuted that statement, at least within myself, because the church building is seldom filled, except at Easter and Christmas. During those two seasons, perhaps the church is full of hypocrites.

Jesus' statements to the Pharisees usually were filled with anger. I wonder if part of our failure to notice the anger in a passage like Mark 3:5 and Matthew 23:13-36 results from our denial of any kinship with the Pharisees. I have noticed that anger directed at someone else never seems as intense as anger directed at me. One of the most effective ways to listen and learn from Scripture is to read a passage putting ourselves in the places of the characters. We need to read the above passages as if we were scribes and Pharisees, because often we are. In reading the Bible, if we identify with the good guys, we probably are misreading the Bible. Read Matthew 23:13-36 pretending to be a

Pharisee hearing Jesus speak to you. What do you hear? How do you react? What emotion was Jesus feeling and expressing?

Mark recorded the story of Jesus healing a man's withered hand on the sabbath. Immediately, Jesus lost credibility with the Pharisees because Jesus' understanding of God and His attitude about people ran headlong into the understanding and attitude of the Pharisees. From this point on, the Pharisees plotted to destroy Jesus because He was a threat to them. His words and example, if followed, would revolutionize the worship of God and human relationships. The Pharisees said the people were made for the law, and Jesus said the law was made to aid the people in their worship and their living, which were inseparable.

Matthew 23:13-36 reveals how Jesus responded to the hypocrisy of the Pharisees, seeking to redeem them. In its original usage, hypocrite was a theatrical term. It was descriptive of an actor in the Greek theatre and meant "one who puts on an act." Before the development of theatrical makeup, masks were used to represent characters. The masks were attached to long sticks which the actors used to hold the masks in front of their faces. One actor would play several roles and would change characters by changing masks. Using a mask to conceal the actor's identity and to give a visual image of a character was appropriate for the theatre. To praise a Greek actor as an excellent hypocrite would have been a compliment.

The word *hypocrite* was a word rich with meaning in its original usage. It began to be applied to people who put on an act in real life, pretending to be persons they were not. These pretenders became identified as hypocrites. This negative connotation of the word developed, and, eventually, the negative inference became the primary meaning.

By the time of Jesus' ministry in the first century, the negative meaning of "hypocrite" was well established. Jesus did not use this word as a compliment of the religious leaders; rather, it was a word of condemnation on their outward actions and demonstrations that were not synchronized with their inward motivations. Jesus accused the Scribes and Pharisees of being out of sync because they pretended to be what they were not. We would like to conclude that hypocrisy was the struggle of people of another age, but we know that is not true. A statement attributed to E.E. Cummings expresses our struggle. He said that to be nobody but yourself, in a world that is doing its best night and day to make you everybody else, means to fight the hardest battle any human being can fight and never stop fighting.

Jesus sought to respond redemptively to the hypocrisy of the Scribes and Pharisees by what He said to them. As the religious leaders they represented Israel as a whole, not just one party. The seven woes recorded in Matthew 23 have been criticized as being too severe to be attributed to Jesus. Partial explanation for this reaction has been the unwillingness of the church to permit Jesus to be a human being experiencing and expressing anger as an emotional response. Some people have concluded that these seven woes were developed later by the church during a period of bitter conflict with Judaism. Generally, however, the more difficult the text is, the nearer to the original it probably is. Certainly these were harsh words that Jesus spoke. A. T. Robertson called this passage "the thunderbolt of wrath" and points out that Jesus' hardest word falls on the religious leaders of the Jews.[2] Plummer says these words are "like thunder in their unanswerable severity, and like lightning in their unsparing exposure. . . . They illuminate while they strike.[3]

At the outset Jesus was speaking to the crowds and to the disciples (Matt. 23:1-11). He encouraged them to listen and learn from the scribes and Pharisees because they were interpreters of the Law. He authorized their verbal instructions; however, Jesus warned His audience about the life-styles of the scribes and Pharisees. Jesus pointed out that the Pharisees did not live what they taught. Jesus used the image of people enjoying the heavy burden they can load on another's back while they carry nothing themselves.

The Greek word *ouai* translated "woe" is neither a curse nor a simple denunciation. It may express anger or pity. It carries a tone of judgment and also lamentation. These woes were directed toward the religious leaders who were in a position to know better and to do better than they were doing in their teaching and their living. In no way was Jesus angry at all Pharisees, neither was He condemning every Pharisee out of hand. He was condemning those who made the law an end in itself. These woes were delivered to the scribes and Pharisees who were the religious leaders. They were spoken in the presence of the disciples, strongly indicating a warning to His disciples that they were not exempt from committing the same sin.

What angered Jesus was that the Pharisees were giving priority to an object over people. The law was a set of standards serving as guidelines for people in their relationships with God and with each other. Whenever obeying the guidelines became more important than the relationships, then people had sold themselves into bondage rather than receiving liberation. The scribes and Pharisees had become the captors using the law as a chain to hold people as captives.

Jesus' first accusation against us as religious leaders is in the context of the kingdom of God being like a huge banquet room. We stand at the doorway inviting people to come to the banquet. We describe the beauty and joy of what it will be like to be at a party where God is the host. People hearing our description approach the doorway, and just before they step through, we shut the door in their faces from the outside. In shutting them out, we also shut out ourselves. What we are unable to have, we are unwilling for others to experience. We have kept the rules that others have broken, and we are unwilling to allow others to enjoy what we have missed. Religion is more important to us than faith. I use the word *religion* in this context to refer to the visible, external deeds that serve as tangible evidence that we have done some good things and that we have avoided some bad things. Faith is a vital, vibrant trust in God. Our security too often is in obeying rules.

We list the rules we have kept that ought to make us righteous, and they make us self-righteous. A serious illness comes to us, and we wonder why we weren't exempt since we have been faithful church attenders and regular financial contributors to the church. We really prefer a set of regulations that serve as a checklist or a report card of our morality.

Jesus also expressed His anger at those scribes and Pharisees because they went to great emotional and financial expense to win a convert and then made him more legalistic than they were. Often when one who has been required to abide by numerous regulations becomes a member of a congregation that one more extremely partisan in his expectations of others than was required of him. An issue that is alive in several Baptist congregations is the requirement of baptism by immersion for membership in a Baptist church. Some who argue in favor of this requirement with the most venom are those who were required to be immersed again when they joined a Baptist congregation.

In expressing His anger to the Pharisees who believed rules take precedence over people, Jesus interchangeably called them hypocrites and blind guides. Those who profess the value of honesty but practice lying eventually have difficulty determining the difference between fact and fiction. When one gains authority from external sources, an authoritarian stance usually is taken. When questions are raised in areas in which a person has no knowledge or is aware there is a conflict of interest, the tendency is toward dogmatism, rigidity, and legalism. This shallowness and threat to security often is met with words forcefully spoken to convince the speaker more than anyone else.

This approach is dramatically portrayed in Leonard Bernstein's *Mass.* The play opens with the celebrant dressed in a robe similar to that of his congregants. As the play progresses, the celebrant feels it necessary to pretend some things rather than wrestle with questions and doubts. He adds vestments and each time he says, "Let us pray," he speaks louder and angrier. His shallowness and pretending become more frightening and threatening as he continues to seek an external solution to an internal need. He continually adds vestments to cover his emptiness and shallowness and to portray security and confidence. Eventually, he collapses from the weight of all his coverings.

Jesus continued with His illustrations of hypocrisy as He called attention to the stewardship practices of the Pharisees and Scribes. The rule of tithing required bringing a tenth of whatever one produced to the Temple. It was a beautiful way to demonstrate the rhythm of give and take that is essential for the benefit of all creation. Mint, dill, and cumin were raised in an individual's small garden and generally were not considered a part of the produce from which one gave a tithe. However, many Pharisees were superlatively meticulous, and they measured out ten percent of the seeds from these plants which might have totaled the production of one plant.

People today may struggle with whether to tithe on their gross income or their net income. Jesus did not condemn tithing although many wish He had and some act as if He did. What is hypocritical is that we count out the pennies we will drop in the offering plate but give no thought to our failure to give a full day's work for a full day's pay. What is hypocritical is our desire for only one color of people to live in our neighborhoods to maintain our advantageous property value. What is hypocritical is our willingness to pay any price for national security even if it means many will starve, and the world will teeter on the brink of annihilation.

Some of Jesus' most stinging words were spoken to the Pharisees about the times they pretended to be who they were not. The most graphic example Jesus used was the practice of the Pharisees who made certain that the tombs were whitewashed. This was so people could avoid being ceremonially unclean because of contact with the dead. Jesus called the Pharisees whitewashed tombs. Outwardly, they looked neat, but inside they were decaying corpses.

How much time and energy do we invest attempting to appear alive and confident when inside we are decaying, insecure, and unsure? We convince ourselves that we must appear to be someone we are not; otherwise, we will be unacceptable. Rabbi Joseph Libermann told of dreaming one night that he had died and stood before the Judge of all the earth, and in that great moment he was not asked, "Why weren't you Moses, Jacob, David, or Solomon?" Rather, he was asked, "Why weren't you Joseph Libermann?" To be nobody but ourselves is the hardest battle we have to fight. Jesus' anger was directed at the scribes and Pharisees who were losing the battle of being themselves, and in the fray they were clutching desperately to all appearances of righteousness that resulted only in self-righteousness. Jesus was angry at those whose practices contradicted their proclamation. He was angered because the Scribes and Pharisees in no way were attempting to synchronize what they did with what they said.

These woes of Jesus were words He spoke expressing deep, mournful concern for those who were misleading people who trusted them. They were spoken to cut through hypocrisy in an attempt to redeem those who were being hypocritical. Jesus loved His people including the scribes and Pharisees. Some became His followers, but many became His enemies. He was angered by people who were in a position to know better and do better but didn't. He used His anger to expose their false values and misplaced trust, seeking to point them to their only hope. Jesus used His anger in an effort to bring reconciliation to the scribes and Pharisees.

This passage in Matthew is an unadulterated effort by Jesus to respond redemptively to the hypocrites. As we begin reading this segment of Scripture, we are reading about religious leaders of the first century. We finish with the passage long before it finishes with us because at some point within it we begin reading about ourselves. There are areas in our lives where who we appear to be and who we are don't match. What Jesus said to the scribes and Pharisees is spoken to us. His anger exposes our false values and misplaced trust, cutting though our hypocrisy, inviting us to proclaim and practice faith in the living God. These words of Jesus invite us to be redeemed from our hypocrisy. They call us to respond redemptively to those around us whose practice and proclamation do not mesh.

Notes

1. Matthew Black, "Pharisees," *The Interpreter's Dictionary of the Bible* (Nashville: Abingdon Press, 1962) vol. K-Q, pp. 777-778.

2. A. T. Robertson, *Word Pictures in the New Testament* (Nashville: Sunday School Board of the SBC, 1930), vol. 1, p. 181.

3. William Barclay, *The Daily Study Bible Series* (Edinburgh: The Saint Andrew Press, 1958), vol. 2, p. 318.

3
Responding to Prejudice

Luke 7: 36-50

How many F's are there in the following sentence?

Finished files are the result of years of scientif-
ic study combined with the
experience of many years.

Did you find three *F's?* That is how many most people see. Now read the sentence again. How many *F's* did you see this time? Actually there are six *F's.* If you saw less than six you probably missed the *F* in the three *ofs.* You missed three of the *f's* because of a mental blind spot. Blind spots or dark areas in a person's visual field is called scotoma.

Prejudice is caused by scotoma. Blind spots occur in our fields of vision with regard to people. The result is: we see categories rather than people. Blind spots make life easier because we do not have to relate to individuals but can relate to all people in the same manner: all Blacks, all Hispanics, all men, all women, all Baptists, all Jews. Some have larger blind spots than others and may be able to see only two groups: men and women, white and nonwhite, or religious and irreligious people. Whether our blind spots be large or small, we all have them as the reading of the sentence above probably demonstrat-ed. Blind spots are the result of laziness. The lazy, easy way involves either not recognizing our prejudices or recognizing them but doing nothing about them. To enlarge one's visual field requires work. Emo-

45

tionally it requires some of the most difficult work any of us will ever do. As followers of Christ we are called to improve and enlarge our vision.

Prejudice is a primary obstacle to human relationships. Although we usually think of prejudice as the expression of strong emotion against a person or a group of people, prejudice may also be a strong emotion in favor of a group, favorable feelings that are in excess of what the situation merits. We usually describe such action as favoritism. We really are glad for favoritism when we are being favored and willingly receive benefits based on prejudice.

I am a native of Kentucky, and I grew up during part of the Adolph Rupp era. Although there were several colleges and universities across the state, all were second to the University of Kentucky when it came to basketball. Generally speaking, people in Kentucky were for two teams in basketball: the University of Kentucky and whoever was playing Notre Dame. Prejudice was beneath these attitudes. People were prejudiced for Kentucky and their anti-Catholic sentiment was manifested by always being against Notre Dame.

Prejudice obstructs human relationships because people make judgments about others based on sights, sounds, and odors. Whenever I speak, my southern Kentucky accent gives me away. Often people from the Northern United States initially want to keep me at a distance because, according to my accent, I am a red-necked bigot. Generally, people from the Southern United States initially are drawn to me because they conclude that my views and values are just like theirs. Usually, I disappoint both groups, and we have to begin again in relating because prejudice obstructed our relationship.

There are multiple causes of prejudice including jealousy, envy, fear, hatred, insecurity, low self-esteem, and self-righteousness. Whatever motive or emotion fuels prejudice, the basic aim is to treat a person or group of people as worthless, worth *less* than the one who is prejudging. Jesus was angered by prejudice because He saw the injustice that resulted (Matt. 25:31-46). Jesus was forever cutting through prejudice by taking His stand alongside those against whom discrimination was being levied (Luke 7:36-50); 10:25-37; 19:1-10). With the Gospels we have four accounts of the life and ministry of Jesus. Each Gospel bears the signature of its author in the form of distinctives that are characteristic of that writer. I am drawing my examples from Luke's Gospel of Jesus responding to prejudice. His writing style portrays the one who is outcast juxtaposed to the one casting him out. Perhaps Luke's style developed out of his personal experience. Luke was a Gentile, the only Gentile author of Scripture. Maybe his experience of being an outcast gave him a clarity of expression about prejudice. The Lukan passages from which I am drawing instruction can guide us in responding redemptively to racism, professionalism, and sexism.

Responding to Racism
Luke 10:25-37

Nowhere is there evidence that Jesus ever made a decision about a person on the basis of outward appearance. Quite the contrary, Jesus responded to people as people. Jesus' approach was upsetting and disturbing in His culture because people had developed methods of relating and had lumped people into groups. Many of the groups were outcasts. The lepers were unclean because of disease. The shepherds and tanners were unclean because of occupation. The Gentiles and Samaritans were unclean because of race.

The parable of the Good Samaritan is one of Jesus' illustrations of how to cut through racism. Jesus simply told the story, made no moral judgment on the Samaritan, but rather suggested that kindness toward anyone in need is what it means to be a neighbor.

A casual reading of the Bible reveals a prejudiced attitude against the Samaritans. The roots of this racial prejudice ran deep. Samaria was a small section of land between Galilee and Judea. In 720 BC, the Assyrians invaded the Northern Kingdom of Samaria and deported many of the local residents while many Assyrians emigrated to Samaria. Local people married foreigners, which was an unforgivable sin to the Jews. Later, when the Southern Kingdom, Judah, was defeated, many people were sent into Exile and later returned. Upon their return the Samaritans offered their assistance in the reconstruction efforts. The Samaritans were told that no assistance from any impure half-breeds was needed. This was 450 BC. The quarrel was just as bitter and the prejudice just as deep in Jesus' lifetime as it had been nearly five-hundred years earlier. The flames of prejudice had been fanned continually, and the coals of hatred had been kept hot.

Many Jews traveled between Galilee and Judea. Travel time was about three days, but practically every Jew made it a six-day trip. The prejudice against Samaritans was so intense that many Jews would not travel through Samaria. Traveling from Galilee Jews would cross the Jordan River, journey south on the eastern side of the Jordan until they had circumvented Samaria, and then cross the Jordan into Judea. Isn't it amazing how far out of the way racism will take people?

This background makes Jesus' parable of the Samaritan all the more disarming to me. Luke did not tell his readers who was in the audience when Jesus told this story. Luke described Jesus and a teacher of the law in dialogue. As Luke told the story, Jesus answered the lawyer's question, "What shall I do to inherit eternal life?" (v. 25). with a question. Jesus was inspecting the situation to learn what the understanding of his questioner was. Luke said the motive behind the scribe's question was to trap Jesus. How did Luke know that? Did he conclude that from the dialogue which was reported to him? The scribe's question seemed legitimate, religious, and holy. What better question could anyone ask than: "What shall I do to inherit eternal life?"

Perhaps Luke interpreted the question as a trick because a scribe was both student and teacher of the religious law. He would know the answer to such a question. Have you ever asked questions to which you already had answers? Why did you do that? To get attention? To demonstrate your knowledge? To trap the person you were questioning?

Persons who use trick questions to trap another person suffer from scotoma because they can imagine only two possible answers to the question, neither of which will be satisfactory. In the situation with the lawyer, as happened often in Jesus' ministry, Jesus responded with an unexpected alternative. Jesus asked the man how he interpreted the law. Jesus said the man had the right answer. All he had to do was put his answer into practice. This is where the lawyer got edgy. It is where many of us become uncomfortable. Clarence Jordan gave a perceptive translation of this dialogue in the Cotton Patch Version. In it, the lawyer has become the teacher of an adult Bible class.

> "That is correct," answered Jesus. "Make a habit of this and you'll be saved."
> But the Sunday school teacher, trying to save face, asked, "But . . . er . . . but . . . just who is my neighbor?"[1]

He asked the wrong Man that question if he wanted the comfort of the status quo. Jesus was forever pushing back the boundaries of exclusiveness to include more people. In this situation, Jesus told a story. I wonder how many times people said to Jesus, "Just give us a yes or no answer." Jesus never gave only *yes* or *no* answers because in the complexity of the issues with which He dealt, for Jesus to say *yes* was to affirm some things He wanted to deny and to say *no* was to deny some things He wanted to affirm.

Jesus immediately caught the lawyer's attention when He said, "A man was going." This was similar to our introduction, "Once upon a time" or "I want to tell you a story." Stories arrest our attention. About all we have from Jesus' ministry are His illustrations—the stories He told. Jesus was able to wrap instructions within a story in such fashion that when a person repeated the story, the instruction was repeated as well. As the lawyer thought of the man Jesus mentioned, the man was a nebulous anybody. He was not the lawyer's wife, child, friend, client, or colleague. To the lawyer, he was a nameless nobody. Jesus did not reveal the man's race, creed, or color. What was significant to Jesus was that a human being had become the helpless victim of evil.

Barclay called the road from Jerusalem to Jericho "The Bloody Way" because of the numerous crimes that occurred there. The terrain made it possible for robbers to conceal their presence and ambush a traveler. The robbery incident that Jesus described was a common occurrence. The lawyer may have concluded that the traveler should have known better than to travel that road alone. However, such an attitude was of no help to a man who had been wounded and left half dead.

In His story, Jesus did not portray the religious leaders in a positive light. The priest and the Levite were passersby in the face of human need. There were numerous priests in Israel, and they rotated on a weekly basis as leaders assisting the high priest in conducting worship in the Temple. The Levites were Temple helpers and likewise were on a service rotation basis. Because of the number of priests and Levites, the chance to serve in the Temple was a rare occasion.

A person could become ceremonially unclean by contact with anyone or any object that was unclean. This defilement lasted seven days, which would have preempted the priest and the Levite's service in the Temple. Neither of them got close enough to the wounded man to discover if he were alive or dead or whether he was a Samaritan, tanner, or shepherd. These religious men were traveling from worship. They knew the rules and obeyed them. When confronted with a choice between keeping the religious rules and helping a person in need, obeying the rules was an easy choice for the priest and the Levite. They were careful to keep their God consciousness from affecting their social consciousness. The priest and the Levite saw themselves primarily as priest and Levite and hurriedly concluded that the injured man was neither. Since the ditch dweller was not their kind, they felt no responsibility to help him. These two religious leaders did not see themselves as part of all humanity but as having kinship with a small, exclusive portion, those who were like them. The priest and the Levite were exclusionists.

I suspect that when you read this story you identify with the Samaritan. You see yourself taking your stand for goodness, health, and wholeness. I believe that when we read Scripture and identify ourselves with those who did right, we are misreading Scripture. To read the stories of Jesus and see ourselves as doing what is right is evidence that we suffer from scotoma. We know what Scripture says, we love to quote it, but we don't want to live by it.

Jesus used the story of the Samaritan to demonstrate how to respond to racism. Surgery is required to remove the racial prejudice because it is deep seated.

The characteristics of compassion and hospitality present in the Samaritan are essential for us to respond redemptively to racism. Compassion is a developed gift that is modeled for us by others. We experience compassion from those who ministered to us when we were wounded. Compassion is the ability, willingness, and eagerness to look beyond the external circumstances, see the internal need of a person, and put oneself alongside the other person to help carry the burden of another.

This story Jesus told indicates three ways to respond to human need: pity, sympathy, and empathy. The first two responses enable the walls between people to remain and even be built higher. To have pity on another person is to feel sorry for him but with contempt for the one who is pitied because he is regarded as weak or indifferent. The person who has pity says of one who is wounded, "It is a shame that he got hurt. He should have known better than to go there alone." Even knowing better does not remove the pain of being wounded. A person who pities another is unwilling to help the one in need.

During World War II my dad was on the front lines in Germany. An artillery shell exploded near him, and many fragments of shrapnel imbedded his flesh, destroying an eye, the muscle in one arm, and causing other, less serious wounds. After being wounded he called for the assistance of a medic. The medic replied, "I'm a medic, but I'm not coming out there." The medic had pity for my dad, but his pity was of no value to him as a wounded man.

Sympathy means having the sameness of feeling of another. Sympathy is an over-against attitude. The sympathizer verbalizes, "I can tell by looking at you that you hurt, and I wish you didn't hurt so deeply." Nonverbally, the sympathizer says, "I certainly am glad that is not happening to me."

The Samaritan empathized with the injured man. Empathy is the projection of oneself into the life and situation of another in order to understand better what life is like for the other. The Samaritan could see himself left to die, and he knew what he would want. He would want someone—anyone—to stop and help him. The Samaritan was a compassionate person and was willing to stand by the injured man until he was healed. Jesus responded to the injustice of racism by telling about a victim of prejudice who showed compassion. People in and out of the church have labeled this man "the Good Samaritan." In a backhanded way, this seems to say that, out of all the rotten Samaritans, there was one good one. Many of us concede today that we know one decent Black or Hispanic who has done well or some Vietnamese who are really energetic. What we imply is that all of the others in these groups are worthless, at least *worth less* than we are.

In addition to being compassionate, the Samaritan was a person of hospitality. *Hospitality* means to be liberal and generous in disposition and mind. To be hospitable is to be receptive and open to people and their ideas. Hospitality is a virtue that causes people to break through the narrowness of their fears and open their lives to strangers.

Concentration and community are the necessities of hospitality. Whenever a person walks into our lives, he becomes our guest. We must pay attention to the person and not be preoccupied with our needs. When our intentions take over, we ask: "What can I get from this person?" which turns the person into a thing. This attitude is at the heart of racism. Personal worth is colored by skin pigmentation. In our convoluted thinking, too many of us have determined that the less pigmentation the more worth a person has, while those with the darkest pigmentation become the objects of greatest scorn and ridicule. When our intentions rule, we no longer listen to what another is saying. Rather, we consider what we can do with what she is saying. Concentration requires that we be open and engaging toward others in order to create the space for another to be herself and come to us on her terms.

Hospitality requires community. When we are hospitable to people, we provide a friendly space for them where they may feel free to come and go. This approach brings healing because it takes away the false illusion that wholeness can be given by one person to another.

The Samaritan's hospitality was generous, and his compassion was extravagant. He bound up the patient's wounds, set him on his donkey, took him to an inn, and stayed with him through the night. The Samaritan could have stopped much sooner than this and still more than fulfilled any possible rule about obligation to wounded strangers. But the Samaritan went even further. He left money and promised that if more were needed he would settle the account upon his return.

When Jesus finished his story, He asked the lawyer which of the three people acted like a neighbor to the wounded person. Notice the lawyer could not bring himself to say "Samaritan." Instead, he simply said that the one who had helped the injured man had acted neighborly. The roots of racism run deep. Only recently, I learned there are people who will not watch the television program "Different Strokes" because blacks are cast in leading roles and portrayed in a positive light.

Racism cannot be abolished with one story, but contained within this parable are the steps necessary to respond redemptively to racism. First, regardless of skin pigmentation or geographical location, all people are human beings; and, therefore, we are more alike than we are different. Cut us, and we bleed; hurt us, and we cry. All of us have been wounded by life and have needed somebody to "donkey" us back to health. Second, we must develop the tandem characteristics of compassion and hospitality. These virtues enable us to look beyond human externals and see people as persons rather than objects. Today, racism may be the single greatest threat to the world community. We in the church know what to do to respond redemptively to racism. I'm afraid we don't want to live by what Jesus taught through this story.

We just love to quote it. "Whoever knows what is right to do and fails to do it, for him it is sin" (Jas. 4:17).

Responding to Professionalism
Luke 19:1-10

Occasionally, in my presence someone will say, "Well, you know how ministers are." I am tempted to say, "No, I don't know how ministers are. Would you like to tell me?" I know how this minister is, but I don't know how all ministers are. When a person has said, "You don't look like a minister," I have asked, "What is a minister supposed to look like?" The response has usually been, "Older, dark suit, a little longer face." This revealed that the responder was permitting the past to intrude into the present. Not only have I had this done to me, but also I have been guilty of stereotyping.

Out of our experiences, we often have constructed images that accumulate through the years, and then an event triggers an association. We relate to a mental image rather than to a living person. With the development of professionals, there seems to be an increase in stereotyping. Specialization has led people with similar skills into the same profession. Thus, we hear references to military types, doctor types, minister types, media types, or professor types. By categorizing people into groups, we choose the lazy way of relating to an image rather than to a person. The image to which we relate has to do with a profession. We tend to think of and relate to all people who are in the same profession in the same way. This form of prejudice is professionalism.

The Bible contains numerous examples of professionalism. Take Zacchaeus. Jesus' encounter with him speaks volumes about responding redemptively to professionalism.

Soren Kierkegaard told about a traveling circus that set up on the outskirts of a village. About forty-five minutes before the performance was to begin, the tent caught on fire. The clown was the only performer fully dressed. He was sent to the village for help.

The clown did his job well. He told everyone he met of the emergency. He begged them to give assistance, but there was a problem. He was dressed like a clown, and over the years people had developed certain expectations of a clown. Getting people to become fire fighters was not one of those expectations. The villagers thought the clown was clowning. Only when they looked out on the horizon and saw the red glow against the sky did they realize that the clown was a human being bearing an urgent message.

Images constructed out of past experiences caused the villagers to miss an urgent message. To stereotype a person is to deny that person the right to be. It is to deny originality to a person. We quickly forget that God mass produces nothing. Stereotyping is our lazy way of coping with masses of people. We lump them into professions rather than investing the energy to see them as persons.

Jesus continued in His ministry and continued to receive criticism and rejection because He did not fit the stereotype of a rabbi. His disciples plucked heads of grain on the sabbath. He healed people and forgave them of their sins. He ate with publicans and sinners which earned Him the notorious titles of "glutton" and "drunkard" (Matt. 11:19).

Out of Jesus' desire to see people rather than stereotype them, He sought to cut through professionalism. Relating to people solely on their profession reduced individuals to position fillers. One of the more meaningful examples is Jesus' relationship with Zacchaeus. Only Luke told this story, and he didn't tell much. Zacchaeus got a total of ten verses in Luke's Gospel, yet people in and out of the church know his story. Probably more people have sung, "Zacchaeus was a wee little man" than have read Luke's ten verses. Zacchaeus was an outcast. Perhaps it is the outcast in us that draws us to Zacchaeus.

The components of Zacchaeus's story are himself, Jesus, Jericho, tax collecting, a sycamore tree, and lunch. With these six nouns, what kind of a story do you think you could write in 175 words or less? Would your story offer a way to respond redemptively to one who was being stereotyped because of his profession. Would your story have so much human interest? Would your story identify so much with people that they would repeat the story because it was partially their story?

The setting of the story is Jericho. Jericho was an important trade center. Because of its warmth, the Herods made it their winter capital. For miles around Jericho, the air was perfumed by the balsam groves. The Romans carried dates and balsam from Jericho to worldwide trade and fame. Jericho was a trade and travel center which made it a major taxation center in Palestine. The Romans collected the personal and property tax themselves, but they contracted the collection of customs on products to tax collectors. The Romans established the amount of revenue they wanted to receive on products and expected the tax collector to earn his fee by collecting more than the minimum tax. Apparently, there were tax collectors who abused this system and sought to line their pockets with cash from their constituents. Tax collectors generally were more affluent than others in the community. This led to guilt by association. Because of the volume of business, Jericho was a prosperous place for tax collectors. Tax collectors and sinners were mentioned together by the religious leaders, suggesting that tax collectors were the worst of sinners.

Zacchaeus has the lead in this vignette that Luke recorded, Zacchaeus was not separated from tax collecting because he was known and related to only by his profession. The prejudice of professionalism formed a scotoma in people's minds. They had no interest or concern in Zacchaeus as a person. The people knew that Zacchaeus was the chief tax collector. Apparently, he was responsible for a district and had a number of subordinate collectors who were answerable to him. Zacchaeus's name means "pure and righteous one." Either he was the opposite of what his name meant, or he was treated as impure and unrighteous by citizens of Jericho.

Being a Jew and a tax collector caused Zacchaeus to make enemies of both Jews and Gentiles. The Jews detested the Romans for occupying their land. To have one of their own aid the occupation forces made him a visible target for their contempt and ridicule. The Romans wanted only the minimum of dealings with the Jews. They just wanted Zacchaeus to collect the taxes. I suspect Zacchaeus's life was lonely. Frederick Buechner described him as "a sawed-off little social disaster with a big bank account and a crooked job."[2] Zacchaeus was a lonely, abused man. Even if he were honest, his profession made him a social outcast.

As the story goes, Zacchaeus climbed a sycamore tree. Common to that area, this tree was easy to climb because of its low branches. Zacchaeus may have climbed the tree for his own protection. The fact he was mingling in the crowd reveals either his courage or his desperation. Being in the crowd gave people the opportunity to curse and ridicule him, to kick, shove, bruise, and spit on him. Since it was Passover we can assume that the crowd was large. A crowd has no conscience and often will do things that individuals would never consider. People in a crowd will take advantage of a situation where no one will hold them accountable for their actions. Were I Zacchaeus, knowing the hostility that the people felt, I'd have climbed the nearest tree, too.

Zacchaeus's body language of being up a tree, out on a limb, tells us some things about Zacchaeus. He wanted to hide but so he could be found. His perch made him aloof from others when what he needed and wanted was to be related to as a person. He was angered and frustrated by the professionalism that stereotyped him. Zacchaeus was a person, but people related to him as a tax collector. He was up a tree emotionally as well as physically.

Zacchaeus was hiding to be found, and Jesus saw him. What caused Jesus to see Zacchaeus? From what we know of Jesus, He doesn't sound like the kind of Person who walked along gazing into space. Maybe from a distance Jesus saw a man in a tree. Jesus was extremely observant of people's needs. People who are on the fringes often stand out to a person who is sensitive to human need. Maybe someone in the crowd pointed to Zacchaeus as a joke and said, "Look who we treed, the old tax collector! We might not let him down." Or perhaps Zacchaeus shook the branches to get Jesus' attention. He wanted to see Jesus. Who of us has not gone to see a well-known person carrying within us the secret desire that the celebrity will see us? Zacchaeus might have been hiding, but like all of us, he wanted to be found.

There Zacchaeus was, peering out between the leaves and branches. Jesus looked up. Their eyes met. What would you have expected Jesus to say? "Who are you?" "What are you doing up there?" "What is wrong with you?" Who would have imagined that Jesus would say, "Zacchaeus, it's lunchtime and I want to eat at your house"? Jesus responded to the professionalism by relating personally to Zacchaeus as an individual rather than as a member of a group.

How would you have responded to Jesus' self-invitation? "This guy has His nerve, inviting Himself to my house!" "Oh, my! With all of these people around, He wants to come to my house for lunch." "I wonder who else He will invite to my house?" "Doesn't He know there is not a thing in the refrigerator?" How did Zacchaeus respond? He left smoldering bark in his wake as he shinned down the tree. As his feel hit the ground he said, "My house is this way."

Jesus identified with Zacchaeus. He stepped across the line that separated them and stood beside Zacchaeus. That is how He responded to professionalism. Then the prejudice of professionalism was used against Jesus. Jesus was a rabbi, a teacher. He had shown promise and insight, but His decision to go home with Zacchaeus revealed this Rabbi's lack of wisdom. Zacchaeus was a sinner. The way sinners were to be treated was to tree them, isolate them, and make them miserable until they hanged themselves or yelled "uncle." If they yelled "uncle," maybe then they would change their ways and earn the right to be part of humanity. The religious leaders understood sinners to be of such a nature that if a person rubbed against them, the sinners would rub off on the righteous rather than the righteous influencing the sinners. The safe approach was to put sinners in social quarantine.

Jesus approached relationships to people differently than His religious contemporaries. If two people had one common characteristic, that did not mean they were identical, and Jesus did not relate to them in the same manner. Michelangelo was once seen rolling a huge rock down the street. When asked what he was doing, Michelangelo replied, "There is an angel in here just waiting to come out." Jesus saw in Zacchaeus a peculiar treasure. He did not see a tax collector; rather, Jesus saw a man who happened to be a tax collector, who needed a friend. The peculiar treasure in Zacchaeus was what he had in him at his best because ultimately it was not the world that had made him.

No record is available of the luncheon conversation between Jesus and Zacchaeus. Surely more was said than what Luke tells; otherwise, Jesus didn't get the first bite of His meal before Zacchaeus was making wild promises to give half of what he had to the poor and to repay four times over the amount he had stolen from anyone. This kind of response must have been based on more than the mere fact that Jesus recognized Zacchaeus and went to lunch with him. If Zacchaeus's response had been reactive gratitude, then it would have been shallow and short-lived. However, Jesus' words after lunch confirmed that not only were words exchanged, but a life was changed. "Today salvation has come to this house" (Luke 19:9).

Jesus responded redemptively to the prejudice of professionalism by taking his stand alongside Zacchaeus. Jesus laid down His life when He went home with Zacchaeus. Jesus died figuratively when He ate with Zacchaeus. What Jesus did so contradicted the religious values of Jericho that it rendered Him vulnerable to rejection and death.

Luke did not tell Zacchaeus's story only as a onetime event. The story is an illustration of what can happen to all of the sawed-off social disasters who walk around in every generation. We may use professionalism as well as having it used to create distance and loneliness. We are the religious in crowd, and it is our self-righteousness that puts us out on a limb. When we look at Zacchaeus, we seldom see any resemblance to ourselves. We don't collect taxes, we pay them. We stand on our one-issue soap boxes to conceal our spiritual shortness. No crowd keeps us from seeing and hearing a celebrity; we just turn on the television. We have worked hard to earn respectability, and we've told our families not to disgrace us. What other people think about us is just about—if not—the most important thing in the world.

Our perspective is very practical and down to earth rather than from
any height overlooking a larger portion of life. Our camouflage is
much more sophisticated than sycamore leaves. We hide ourselves so
well behind the faces we wear that we often don't know who we are.
We have done so many wonderful things that if we could just get Jesus
to eat lunch with us, we would talk his ear off for thirty minutes
repeating all our accomplishments. The silence would drive us up a
tree and out on a limb. Then Jesus' eyes would meet ours, and we
would hear Him say, "I love you; I accept you. You are a treasure
for what you are at your best, because I know who made you who you
are."

Actually, we are more like Zacchaeus than a surface acquaintance
reveals. Zacchaeus was unrighteous. We are self-righteous, pointing
out to ourselves, and often to others, all the help we are to God. The
unrighteous and the self-righteous arrive at the same point from
opposite directions. Both are lost. *Lost* in New Testament usage
means in the wrong place. A person is lost when he or she has
wandered away from God and is misplaced. Professionalism can separate one from God or keep a person at a distance from God. This
happens either when a person sees himself only as a professional—
playing a role—or by others relating to the person as a professional,
rather than as one person to another.

Unrighteous persons are lost because they find their identity to be
less than God created. They make no claim at being righteous and
cannot be blamed for not having achieved righteousness. Self-righteous persons are lost because they find their identity by attempting
to be more than God created. Self-righteous persons set the standards
to be kept according to what they are able to accomplish. They abide
by their own standards, ridiculing those who don't, can't, or won't live
by them.

Jesus responded redemptively to all of this professionalism with one
look and one statement to Zacchaeus. In essence He said, "Let's be
friends." He suggested that Zacchaeus quit acting like a bird or a treed
animal, come down, and be human. When Zacchaeus was treated

differently, he acted differently. Jesus saw and related to the person rather than the profession. Jesus found the person, Zacchaeus.

Responding to Sexism
Luke 7:36-50

"Women are more like men than anything else in the world. They are human beings."[3] The Gospel accounts of Jesus' life and ministry reveal clearly that Jesus related to women as persons to be accepted and loved rather than as objects to be used. The Samaritan woman at the well, the woman caught in adultery, and Mary Magdalene are extensive illustrations. The account of the woman who anointed Jesus' feet provides the detailed way that Jesus responded redemptively to sexism.

Some of Luke's distinctive interests are contained in this story. He revealed Jesus' sociability and enjoyment of hospitality, the worth of all people to Jesus, His love toward sinners, and His forgiveness of sins. Mark and John record a similar story but with differences.

Jesus was invited to the home of a Pharisee whose name is not revealed until later in the story. The invitation included dinner. In those days people reclined on couches on their sides to eat their meals with their feel extended away from the table. Part of the Eastern custom when a teacher was invited to dinner was for people to come in from the street at their leisure and listen to the conversation. A woman came in from the street who apparently knew Jesus or knew about Him. She came prepared to anoint His feet.

Luke's style is to contrast the insider and the outsider. In the first sentence of this story Luke introduced the Pharisee (the insider) and the sinful woman (the outsider). In rabbinic literature the phrase "sinful woman" is used to identify a prostitute. This woman's sin is not disclosed, but it may have been prostitution. In a male-oriented world, prostitutes were despised as sinners. Men could retain their respectability even though they patronized prostitutes.

Jesus received numerous invitations to dine with a variety of people. Apparently, He accepted every invitation that was offered and initiated some of His own (Luke 19:5). In the play *Harvey,* an acquaintance says to the lead character, "Let's have dinner sometime." Immediately the lead whips out his pocket calendar and says, "How about Tuesday evening at seven?" I sense that whenever an invitation was extended to Jesus, He accepted it. Because He didn't discriminate with whom He ate, Jesus was discriminated against. One of the highest compliments paid to Jesus was first uttered in derision: He eats with tax collectors and sinners (see Matt. 9:11).

Jesus went to a Pharisee's home for dinner. Immediately, Luke portrayed the contrast between the Pharisee and the woman through the hospitality customs of the day. There were three things which a host usually did for his guest. When the guest arrived, the host would place his hands on the guest's shoulders and give a kiss of greeting that symbolized the guest was welcome in the host's home. Travel was done by walking in sandals, and the roads were dirt. When a guest arrived in a home, the host would wash the guest's feet, a refreshing gesture as well as a symbol of the host being a servant to the guest. After the guest was refreshed, perfume or olive oil was put on the guest's head. The Pharisee did none of these. No reason is given for the oversight. Jesus was not a traditionalist, and He expected no one to keep a custom just to be observing it. However, indirectly the Pharisee made an issue out of his own oversight.

Apparently, this woman had seen Jesus and had some understanding of who He was and what He could do. She came in from the street and stood behind Jesus at His feet. The context of this event caused her emotions to overflow. There she stood, sobbing. She noticed her tears were making circles in the dust on Jesus' feet as they dropped from her cheeks. She stooped down and dried Jesus' feet with her hair. No one, certainly no man, had ever treated her like a person, like she was somebody, that is, no man except Jesus. Her tears flowed. This woman became so caught up in what was happening to her that she forgot where she was. She dried Jesus' feet with her hair. A woman was never to let her hair down in public, figuratively or literally. This woman had done both because in the words of the hymn she had become "lost in wonder, love, and praise."

After she had dried Jesus' feet, she broke a bottle of nard (Mark 14:3). Nard was a very expensive perfume that came from India. The cost of it was equal to a year's salary in that time. The fact that the woman broke the bottle is an indication that all of the expensive perfume was to be used. There was a custom in the Eastern culture that if a glass were used by a distinguished guest, then it was to be broken, so no one less than he would ever use it. Perhaps this was part of the woman's symbolism in breaking the bottle.

This entire event disturbed the Pharisee's images of himself and of Jesus. The Pharisee was accustomed to men stopping by to overhear conversation but not women, certainly not a sinful woman like this one. What about his reputation? What would his friends and colleagues think when they heard about this? Just as disturbing to this Pharisee was how he had been fooled by Jesus. He had been intrigued by Jesus' sharp, intelligent, insightful ability and approach.

The Pharisee began to question whether or not Jesus was a prophet. Simon figured that an authentic prophet would not allow himself to be ritually unclean by allowing himself to be touched by one who was unclean. The Pharisee talked to himself about what Jesus was permitting. I don't know who told Luke what the Pharisee said. However, the Pharisee drew one conclusion: Jesus was no prophet. Numerous other conclusions could have been drawn such as: "Jesus certainly is kind to this woman," or "This woman is struggling with an important issue in her life," or "Jesus doesn't seem to be disturbed by this woman's presence and attention." The Pharisee suffered from scotoma about the woman. He had a prejudged opinion of her, and he found support for his view. Then the Pharisee put Jesus in the category with the woman. If Jesus could not discern what kind this woman was, then Jesus must be her kind and no prophet. The Pharisee concluded, *You can tell a person by the company he keeps.*

No dialogue between the Pharisee and Jesus had been recorded to this point. Luke inserted that the Pharisee talked to himself, and Jesus answered him. How did Jesus know what the Pharisee was thinking? Perhaps Jesus read minds. Maybe they had been in conversation, and the Pharisee's words trailed off. Perhaps his eyes wandered. Haven't you been in a conversation when you could tell by the eyes that the other person was not listening? Maybe the Pharisee's eyebrows assumed a harsh expression, or his jaw got stern, or his lips quivered as he mumbled to himself. In any case, Jesus sensed the Pharisee's withdrawal.

Jesus immediately arrested the Pharisee's attention by calling his name. Wherever the Pharisee had gone on his mental excursion, Jesus brought him back to the table when He said, "Simon." The quickest way to get a person's attention is to call the person's name. Jesus did this and then held Simon's attention by raising his curiosity, "I have something to say to you" (v. 40). What was He going to say? Jesus said two people were in debt, one owed ten times more than the other. Both accounts were marked paid in full by the lender. Which one will love the lender more? Simon had the right answer, the one forgiven more. He was used to having the right answers.

Jesus got Simon's attention and engaged him in conversation. Then came the confrontation. Looking at the woman, a method Jesus used to direct Simon's attention to her, Jesus asked, "Do you see this woman?" (v. 44). What a ridiculous question! Obviously, Simon had seen her; otherwise, why had he done all that talking to himself about Jesus not being a prophet? Was not Jesus' question an expression of anger directed toward Simon because he had stereotyped the woman? Simon did not answer the question because his answer would incriminate him. He had not "seen" the woman: he had stereotyped her. He knew her kind. He knew how to relate to her kind: have nothing to do with her! He saw her as an object used by men for their pleasure and benefit. Now Simon used her for his benefit; he used her as a yardstick to measure how good he was compared to her.

Then Jesus contrasted the action of the woman with the lack of action by Simon. Why did Jesus underscore the hospitality customs that Simon had overlooked? Was it because Simon insisted on going by the rules regarding a sinful woman? Often the most consistent thing about insistent rule keepers is their inconsistency or their selectivity about which rules to keep. Some of those who have insisted most strongly that businesses close on Sunday have been the most frequent patrons of restaurants for Sunday lunch following worship services.

Rule keepers insist on retribution if not revenge. They seem to gain satisfaction in using the rules to break those who break the rules. Simon the Pharisee illustrated this with his attitude toward the woman. Invariably, Jesus saw the person and then saw their potential which had been locked up by guilt, prejudice, or oppression. It is told that Willis Sutton once decided to read the Gospels as if they were entirely new to him. When he had finished, his wife asked him what he found new in them. He said he was impressed that Jesus never met an unimportant person.

The way Jesus related to this unknown woman in Simon's house was characteristic of the way Jesus related to all women and all men. Every person was of worth and importance as a person. Jesus saw the uniqueness of the individual and related to each person's uniqueness. In Jesus' culture, women were considered property and were so treated. Single adult women in Jesus' day had three strikes against them: being a woman, being unmarried, and having no children. Jesus related to women and treated them as people of worth and value. Examples include Jesus' relationship with the woman caught in adultery (John 7:53 to 8:11) and the woman at the well in Samaria (John 4:1-42). In this latter example Jesus crossed several lines of separation. He as a man talked theology openly with a woman. He as a Jew asked to drink from the ritually unclean bucket of a Samaritan. Added to this was the awkwardness of the woman's marital situation. In this situation as in others, Jesus did not defer to the woman because she was a woman. He asked of her a drink, and He offered her a drink of living water. Jesus saw this woman as a person rather than as a woman, a Samaritan, or a sinner. Thus Jesus responded and related redemptively to women.

One Revolution after Another
Galatians 3:15-29

The life and ministry of Jesus were remarkable and revolutionary. Almost as revolutionary was the early history of the church. One of the most revolutionary statements ever penned is this, "There is neither Jew nor Greek, there is neither slave nor free, there is neither male nor female; for you are all one in Christ Jesus" (Gal. 3:28). Does not this statement summarize both church history and church mission?

The major source of conflict in the early church was the inclusion of Jews and Gentiles into the church on an equal basis. One of Peter's breakthroughs came via a dream prior to his visit with Cornelius. Through the dream Peter was converted from his racist stance of thinking that some things and/or some people God had made were unclean. We, like Peter, have not allowed the good news to permeate every nook and cranny of our lives. There are parts of us that remain unconverted. Out of those areas arise tension, conflict, and resistance fueled by prejudice.

The apostle Paul became convinced that non-Jews were as important to God as Jews were. Paul arrived at this conviction after encountering Christ on the Damascus Road and after spending three years in the Arabian desert. He devoted himself to the task of being minister to the Gentiles. He wrote, "There is neither Jew nor Greek, . . . for you are all one in Christ Jesus." This attitude was revolutionary in the thinking and living of human relationships. It took over two-thousand years for the religious community to face this issue which remains unresolved for many in the world today.

Paul made a second revolutionary statement—"There is neither slave nor free." Whenever and wherever this statement was uttered and practiced in the first century, it was revolutionary. This attitude upset the economy, broke down the balance of power, and changed the ways people related to each other. In the first century, slavery was prominent in the Roman Empire. Paul wrote that for a slave owner to commit himself to Christ would alter the way he related to his slaves. The next step would be to annihilate slavery.

Annihilating slavery met with great resistance in the United States. Slavery had been woven into the fabric of society and culture. Slavery was the major issue that resulted in the splitting of denominations, families, and our country. These people had heard, "There is neither slave nor free," but many applied it to another life in another time. This revolution has been going on for two-thousand years, and it has not been resolved completely.

In the early 1960s a young man came from Nigeria to the United States to earn a college education. Through the work of missionaries this young black man had become a Christian. He wanted to become a minister and return to his native land. He enrolled as a student at Georgetown College in Kentucky. While at college he wanted to be active in a local church. He presented himself for membership in a local church of the missionary's denomination, but membership was denied because he was black. Here was a congregation caught in the contradiction of proclaiming equality but practicing prejudice.

Evidence of racism and professionalism remains in the 1980s. Revolutions caused by the attitude that there is neither Jew nor Greek, neither slave nor free continue. These two revolutions have not been resolved completely. Obvious to the most casual observer is evidence that we are in the midst of the third relational revolution in church history: "There is neither male nor female."

Jesus elevated women to a place of equality and mutuality with men which is the place where they had been when God created humanity in His image, making them male and female. Many women were important in the life of the early church. Mary Magdalene was the first witness and proclaimer of the resurrection of Christ. Priscilla was a missionary. Lydia was a businesswoman and one of the founders of the church in Philippi. Phoebe was a deacon, apparently ordained and set apart for ministry in the church at Cenchreae.

The church has been quick to give to women the responsibility of service but slow to give them the responsibility of leadership. The church has claimed ordination as an honor but often has reserved the honor for men only. Many denominations struggle with this issue today. As recently as 1984 my denomination passed a resolution opposing the ordination of women.

Baptist history reveals that women have been given recognized leadership in the church. As early as 1611, women served as deacons in Baptist congregations. John Smyth claimed then that the local church had the power both to elect and to ordain women deacons.[4] A decline in the number of women deacons began to occur in the 1800s. As deaconal functions became more administrative and shifted toward business management rather than caring and supportive ministries, the shift was away from women as deacons.

In recent years the diaconate has been viewed by many as a ministry of practical service. This emphasis along with increased sensitivity to the rights of women in culture and society has resulted in the ordination of women as deacons and ministers. Sensitivity to the rights of women is part of the continuing revolution in which the church needs to be involved and in which the church needs to take the lead.

Jesus met, confronted, and responded redemptively to prejudice practically every day of His ministry. He was angered by the injustice some people suffered because of the scotoma, or blind spots, that others had. Three of the many forms that prejudice took in the first century were racism, professionalism, and sexism. These same forms are prevalent today. Part of the mission of the church is to learn from the Redeemer to respond redemptively to these prejudices seeing people as people rather than stereotyping them according to their racial identity, vocational choice, or sexual identity. The church can model the process of redemptive responses to prejudice by examining and pointing to the life and ministry of Jesus as the model of human wholeness.

Notes

1. Clarence Jordan, *The Cotton Patch Version of Luke and Acts* (New York: Association Press, 1969), pp. 46-47.

2. Frederick Buechner, *Peculiar Treasures: A Biblical Who's Who,* (New York: Harper & Row, Publishers, 1979), p. 180.

3. Dorothy L. Sayers, *Are Women Human?* (Grand Rapids, Mich.: William B. Erdmans Publishing Co., 1971), p. 37.

4. John Smyth, *Paralleles, Censures, Observations* n.d., n.p.

4
Responding to Rejection

Mark 6: 1-13

Have you ever been lonely? Have you ever been blue? Practically everybody would answer *yes* to each of these questions. Aren't you deep down at least a little bit lonely? When was the first time that you felt lonely? Do you know what is the source or cause of your loneliness? Loneliness usually is a mixture of longing and pain. As I write these words I feel a sense of loneliness. Writing, sermon preparation, even sermon delivery is a lonely experience. The longing and the pain are mixed the most intensely for me during sermon delivery. The sermon is very much a part of me. I am vulnerable, extending myself to the congregation. Now they will know exactly what I think and how I feel about this issue or situation. What if they don't like what they hear? Can they disagree with the sermon content without disagreeing with my personhood? Can they reject the sermon without rejecting me?

Longing and pain are mixed in the writing of these words. I long to communicate to you, the reader, and I hope that I have something to say that will be of value and benefit to you. There is pain here as well as I anticipate your response and fear that you will discard anything that I have to say as worthless. Perhaps this is where the pain of loneliness gets its impetus. To be declared worthless, valueless to another person, is devastating for us because as human beings we are relational creatures by nature and by need. We invest an amazing amount of energy attempting to avoid being rejected. Did you know that the two books stolen the most often from the New York Public

70

Library are the Bible and Emily Post?[1] Both books offer to tell us how to stay in relationship with people and with God.

I have had a parishioner or two who concluded that I was worthless to them as their pastor. They were convinced that I had nothing to offer them as their pastor. They were correct. Having arrived at that decision about me and in essence having rejected me as their pastor, there was no way I could be a pastor to them. Although they remained members of the church and continued to participate in the life of the congregation, I had nothing to offer them. This was a painful realization to admit and integrate into my life.

My experiences of rejection may be extremely minor compared to what you have encountered. I always have had some other person around with whom I could talk about the hurts and pains of loneliness. As a child I was not abandoned either emotionally or physically. I have never had my spouse say to me, "My life would be much happier without you as a part of it." No one has ever told me that I was of no value to them or that the world would be a better place if I were not in it. No employer has ever said my services were not wanted anymore or that I was not contributing toward the purpose and goals of the firm. No one ever said I was of no use to the company or that the economy was so bad that my job was being eliminated. You may conclude that I have lived a very sheltered, naive, and Pollyannish life.

I have listened to the stories of people who felt their lives were worthless because of the rejection they experienced from important people in their lives. I have felt their pain and have attempted to aid them in dealing with the rejection and in integrating their pain into their lives. This is a long and difficult process. One of the coping mechanisms that develops quickly for a person who has been rejected is to reject others before they can reject her.

A more wholesome approach is to find ways to respond redemptively to the rejection we experience rather than rejecting others before they reject us. Redemptive response to rejection is an involved, difficult, and treacherous process. The process is best facilitated with the assistance of another person in whom trust and confidence are established and grow. Nothing angered Jesus any more than the rejection of the tax collectors and sinners by the scribes and Pharisees. Jesus reached out to those who were rejected and included them in His life. He also attempted to include the rejectors in His circle of relationships, but they often wanted to have nothing to do with Him. There is guidance for us in being reconcilors to the rejected in the way that Jesus dealt with the personal rejection that He experienced.

Times Jesus Was Rejected

The pages of the Gospels are filled with illustrations of times when Jesus was rejected. He found Himself almost in constant conflict with the religious establishment and leadership of His day. As a result, His ideas, teachings, and methods were continually being bombarded as unorthodox. He was labeled a rule breaker, a lawbreaker, and therefore a troublemaker.

Three incidents stand out as potent illustrations of the blantant rejection that Jesus experienced personally. No doubt the first two of these experiences made significant contributions to Jesus' ability to face and deal with the third. The first two situations also give some insight into Jesus and the development of His sensitivity to others who were being rejected.

The first rejection that I mention is recorded in John's Gospel (John 1:43-51). This passage records the call of Philip and Nathanael to be disciples. Only in John do we learn about Nathanael. He is not mentioned in the other Gospels, although tradition holds that he and Bartholomew were the same person. In any event, Philip announced to Nathanael, "We have found him of whom Moses in the law and also the prophets wrote, Jesus of Nazareth, the son of Joseph" (v. 45). The irony is that Philip did not find Jesus; rather Jesus found Philip. Is that not the way it is with God? God comes to us. God finds us. We do not find God. Long before we ever give any thought to seeking, knowing, or loving God, God already is seeking, knowing, and loving us.

Can you imagine the rise and fall of excitement that Nathanael experienced? Philip came with such an important announcement, "We have found Him!" The reference is to the Messiah. Many Jews were looking for the Messiah, expecting Him to come. The more devout Jews looked for and longed for the coming of the Messiah more devoutly. Because of their concern for the coming of the Messiah, many questions had arisen about the Messiah's arrival. How would He come? From where would He come? When would He come? On more than one occasion, someone had attempted to answer the latter question only to be disappointed. However, many were convinced of the answers to the first two questions. They were certain that the Messiah would come as a military leader, that He would come from the family of David, and therefore from Judah. Since David was their most revered king, the people were convinced that the Messiah would come from David's family line, and Judah would be His family's homeland.

The surge of excitement in Nathanael must have been nearly uncontrollable when Philip said, "We have found Him!" Just as quickly as the excitement had risen in Nathanael it escaped him. It was like puncturing a balloon with a pin when Philip said, "Jesus of Nazareth, the son of Joseph." The disappointment was so great that Nathanael could not contain himself. Without even thinking, Nathanael blurted out his reaction, "Can anything good come out of Nazareth?" (v. 46). What a prejudiced response! What a mind-set about the Messiah and from where He had to come! In essence Nathanael said, "When the Messiah comes, He may come from any town or village except Nazareth."

If Philip had said, "Jesus of Cana," Nathanael might have considered that as a possibility since he was from Cana. The rivalry between villages was intense. As with most rivalries, one of the ways of feeling superior is to put down the rival. Perhaps Nathanael was voicing the contempt of Cana for Nazareth. It is more likely, however, that Nathanael reacted as a serious student of the Scriptures who knew that no son of Joseph ever had been anticipated in the promises of Scripture.

Philip did not argue with Nathanael. That is a guiding principle for us. Very little is accomplished through argument other than the entrenchment of the arguers in their own opinions. Philip simply invited Nathanael to come and see for himself.

How would you react if you had been in Jesus' situation? What if someone said upon being introduced to you, "I have never believed that anything good could come out of your hometown, and meeting you has confirmed what I have always believed." In essence this is what Nathanael said about Jesus. Contrast Jesus' response to Nathanael with Nathanael's comment about Jesus. Jesus took one look at Nathanael and said, "Here is a real Israelite; there is nothing false in him!" (v. 47, GNB). Jesus was not using flattery. Jesus was being honest about how He perceived Nathanael.

Jesus functioned on the basis that honesty and openness contributed more to healthy dialogue and growth than flattery, sarcasm, facetiae, or psychological games. Jesus confronted Nathanael with His deepest sense of identity, with the style of life that he sought most passionately to emulate. How did Jesus know so much about Nathanael? We need not see Jesus as clairvoyant at this point. Jesus said that He had seen Nathanael under his fig tree. Whether this was meant to be literal or symbolic, it depicted the spiritually ideal conditions under which to study the law of God (Mic. 4:4; Zech. 3:10). Jesus took the Scriptures seriously, and He attached the utmost significance to a sincere study of Scripture by those who earnestly sought the messianic reign of peace (John 5:39-46). Jesus' honest, insightful, open acceptance of Nathanael cut through Nathanael's rejection of Jesus. Nathanael's rejection quickly gave way to acceptance and faith as he exclaimed, "Rabbi, you are the Son of God! You are the King of Israel!" (v. 49).

Acceptance of others is a redemptive response to rejection. People who have been rejected find it very difficult to believe that anyone will accept them and believe in them. Often their hostility at having been rejected is sprayed at anyone who hints at accepting them. This defense mechanism is a means of testing the authenticity of the relationship.

I was in a marriage-growth group many years ago. During several sessions of sharing and relating, one woman seemed intent on castigating every man in the group. One night as I listened to her, I had the image of a woman who was rolling out the barrels of hostility to see if anyone would jump over them and reach her, or would all of us allow the barrels to bowl us over and keep us at a distance from her? I took a chance and told her of my image. With tears in her eyes she said I was right, and the source of much of her hostility was the rejection she felt from her father who had abandoned her and her mother when she was a child. Accepting her turned out to be a redemptive response to the rejection that she had experienced.

The second incident of Jesus being rejected on which I want to focus is the well-known situation at the Nazareth synagogue. This event is recorded in the Synoptics, but its place in Jesus' ministry is different in Luke than in Matthew and Mark. Luke (4:16-30) recorded this event in Jesus' life as at the beginning of His ministry. Luke was the only one of the Synoptic writers to identify the place as Nazareth explicitly. Matthew and Mark inferred it to be Nazareth by writing that Jesus came to His own country. In Matthew and Mark's arrangement of events, Jesus had been engaged in ministry in Galilee. He traveled to Nazareth and went to the synagogue on the Sabbath as was His custom (Luke 4:16). Jesus taught in the synagogue. Any Jewish man could be invited to teach in a synagogue. Many people were there when Jesus taught, and they were ambiguous in response to His teaching. First they were amazed, then annoyed and irritated.

The people were amazed at Jesus' wisdom. Why? Apparently, it was because Jesus was a hometown boy, and many of those at the synagogue had watched Jesus grow up. They could not comprehend how someone they had seen toddling around could now know more than they. This could not be authentic wisdom because they knew His family. Wisdom could not possibly come from someone they already

knew. Anything worthwhile must come from afar. Besides Jesus was
a carpenter. What could a lowly craftsman know about religion, the
law, and the higher things of life? In addition He was the son of Mary.
This was an unusual identification. Usually, a boy or man was identified with his father. Some have suggested that this identification
indicated that Joseph had died while Jesus was young, and that identifying Jesus as the carpenter indicated that He had taken on the
responsibility of providing for the family.

I wonder if identifying Jesus as the son of Mary were not a slur on
His background and a question about the manner of His birth. After
all, when Mary's due date had arrived, she had left town with Joseph
to go to Bethlehem for the census. If there had not been some question
about the legitimacy of her pregnancy, why wouldn't she have stayed
at home where she could have had the assistance of women she knew?
Were those who identified Jesus as the son of Mary seeking to discred-
it any wisdom He had offered by tainting His reputation because of
the circumstances of His birth? I think so. Those who have known a
person the longest do not necessarily know a person the best. Innuen-
do is a common method of attack toward one who is a threat to
another's position or popularity. We hear it often in political cam-
paigns. In some ways, the situation with Jesus was a political cam-
paign as far as the religious leaders were concerned.

The townspeople of Nazareth were not prepared to receive wisdom
from one who had grown up among them. Jesus may have seemed
unusually gifted to them, but His heritage was utterly ordinary. The
people were unable to bring themselves to believe that God might be
at work among them, particularly in one of such humble and, in the
eyes of some, questionable origin. The family of Jesus as well as the
citizens of Nazareth apparently did not support Jesus in His ministry.
Why do those who are the closest to someone emotionally have the
greatest difficulty with the person's vocation and accomplishments?
The answers seem to be resentment, jealousy, and envy. The villagers
of Nazareth took offense at Jesus. Were they not envious and resentful
that Jesus was gaining attention and offering insight to people? Did

they not wish that the attention and popularity which Jesus seemed to be receiving were coming to them? In another context Jesus said, "Blessed is he who takes no offense at me" (Matt. 11:6). Rare is the person who can see the ability and accomplishment of someone he has known for a long time and celebrate and congratulate that person with authentic joy.

Oscar Wilde told a story about a religious hermit. His commitment as a Christian was so strong that the evil spirits sent to tempt him ended up defeated and discouraged. They were unable to break him down. They tried passions of the body and doubts of the mind. They even tried to provoke pride in his goodness. Every temptation failed. Finally, Satan himself came to the evil spirits and said, "Your methods are crude. Permit me one moment." Satan went to the hermit and asked, "Have you heard the good news? Your brother has been made bishop of Alexandria." That got to him! "My brother, bishop of Alexandria!" And the tidal wave of envy swept over him.

Envy was at work in the lives of those Nazareth villagers. Not only did they regret and despise Jesus' success and recognition by others, but also they were eager for some misfortune to befall Him. Frederick Buechner has defined envy as the consuming desire to have everybody as unsuccessful as you are.[2] Envy goes even further. Envy says that if I can't be better than you, then I will destroy you, so you will not have a chance to be better than I. Envy was at work in the lives of the villagers of Nazareth as Jesus sought to teach in the synagogue. Jesus was neither a trained scribe nor a professional rabbi; he was a layman. Who knows which was more troublesome to the villagers, that Jesus was untrained or that people responded to Him? Certainly the experts in religion were horrified, scandalized, and insulted that this untrained Galilean dared to teach and received such a positive response everywhere except in Nazareth.

Certainly, the most devastating and destructive experience of rejection that Jesus encountered was the cross. Rejection there literally became a life-and-death issue. In many ways what Jesus experienced in the synagogue in Nazareth was a foreshadowing of the cross. The rejection that Jesus experienced in Nazareth expanded during His three-year ministry and culminated in His crucifixion. On the cross He felt the rejection of the crowd who only a few days earlier had cheered His arrival in Jerusalem. A thief who was being rejected by the society found a target in Jesus onto whom he projected his own rejected feelings by scornfully attacking Jesus, attempting to get Jesus to prove who He was. The soldiers taunted Him and made fun of Him. Earlier, one of His disciples had betrayed Him, and another denied any knowledge of Him. Both were extremely personal forms of rejection. At the cross, nearly everyone rejected Jesus. Each person by overt action or lack of action declared Jesus' life as worthless and valueless. That is what it means to be rejected, and the cross is the cruelist symbol of rejection in all of history because of Whose rejection it represents.

Ways Jesus Responded to Rejection

In these three incidents of rejection in Jesus' life, there are redemptive methods of responding to rejection that are common to each of the situations. In each incident, Jesus' first move was to acknowledge and accept the rejection. He seemed to name, at least to Himself, what He was feeling and what was happening to Him. This approach is as ancient as the Garden of Eden in Genesis where human beings were given responsibility for naming the animals. Naming the animals gave people some control over them.

Once Jesus acknowledged and accepted the rejection that was being directed toward Him, He was then able to accept the persons doing the rejecting. In Nathanael's case, Jesus' acceptance of Nathanael turned him around. He began living life in a different direction when he was treated differently by Jesus than he was treating Jesus. There are numerous situations where this is true today. Teachers often find this approach helpful in relating to and dealing with difficult students who seem to be bent on rejecting others before others reject them. Parents have found this approach to be essential in facing the parenting challenge of relating to their children. Counselors also have found this approach helpful.

An incident I had with a counselee will illustrate the point. I had had three appointments with a thirty-three-year-old woman who was having serious motivational problems related to her job. She was depressed and had been brought to me by a church member. At the time for her fourth appointment, I was detained at the hospital and was fifteen minutes late for the appointment. Although I had left clear instructions that I would be there for the appointment but would be late, when I arrived, Joan [not her real name] was not there. Two days later I received a telephone call from her. She was extremely angry with me. She wanted to know what the situation was with me. Would I show up the next time? Would there be a next time? What was I trying to do to her? She said she had a good notion to come to the church on Sunday and create a scene, but she thought maybe it was better to call me since I had not called her. I made an appointment with her and assured her that I would be there. I also assured her that I was present for the last appointment, but she did not wait as I had asked that she do. I arrived ten minutes early for the next appointment, and Joan was already there. I suspect that if I had been only five minutes late this time, she would have left before I arrived.

During this session, I gained some significant insight into Joan's life. She began having seizures when she was six and had to take medication to control them. Her mother became extremely protective of Joan and would not let her go anywhere by herself, such as down the road to the neighbor's house. Joan was not told until she was thirteen that she had epilepsy. Her parents had only told her that she had to take the medication, but they never answered her directly when she had asked for what she was taking medicine. There were many times at school when she threw away the medicine but assured her mother that she had taken it. When she was thirteen, her parents arranged to take her to a hospital for tests to determine if a new medication would be more helpful. Joan did not want to go. Her parents insisted and told her that she would be there only a day or two, and they would stay with her. When they got her to the hospital, Joan's parents left her for a week. She recalls yelling and screaming up and down the halls. She would call home, and, finally, her parents would hang up the telephone. She was convinced they were never coming back for her.

As a result of this experience, Joan became emotionally frozen, and she tended to relate to nearly every person out of this experience. Joan is convinced that nobody cares about her. At the slightest hint in her perception that someone does not want to relate to her, Joan rejects the person before that person ever has a chance to reject her. That was why she did not wait fifteen minutes on me for an appointment. In her mind she was convinced that I did not want to have anything else to do with her. Of course, her dumping her anger on me, and being unfair to me from my perspective, caused me to respond with anger and not wanting to invest time and energy with her. The temptation was to reject her by terminating the counseling relationship. And once again rejection would have become a self-fulfilled prophecy for Joan.

The old adage that sticks and stones may break my bones, but words can never hurt me is false. Words are vehicles that carry messages and feelings between people. The words and the lack of them between Joan and her parents have hurt her deeply. The scars will remain with her all of her life. In working with Joan, I wanted to help heal the wound of rejection she had felt so that an open emotional sore would not remain to drive away people to whom Joan wanted and needed to relate.

To be rejected in a relationship causes a person to be insecure about relating to another person in a similar situation. The insecurity often causes a tentative reaction in the other person which the insecure person reads as rejection. Fear of being rejected causes one often to act as if she has been rejected which results in someone rejecting her. The vicious cycle continues.

For one who has been rejected to accept those who have done the rejecting is neither an easy accomplishment nor does it always net the positive results that Jesus had with Nathanael.

Jesus' experience in the Nazareth synagogue is a clear example where accepting the rejectors made no positive difference to them. Actually, Jesus' acceptance of them seemed only to be like pouring gasoline on a fire. He acknowledged being rejected by stating, "A prophet is not without honor, except in his own country, and among his own kind, and in his own house" (Mark 6:4). This was a realistic observation by Jesus. This is a general rule of thumb but not a legalistic statement about every prophet from every town. Jesus had a sharp eye and a realistic mind without a trace of paralyzing cynicism. There are no more severe critics than those who have known a person from his childhood. They have seen and tend to remember all of the mistakes that he has made in their eyes. They often are blind to the growth and changes that the person has made through life experiences.

There are many factors that cause people to miss the truth. Some are convinced that if they have all the material facts that they have the truth. Others are convinced that if they can know the origin of an idea or a person, then they have the truth. Still others are convinced that truth must come from a certain social, economic, or intellectual level. If it comes from some other level, they conclude that it must be false. All of this was tied into the rejection that Jesus experienced in the synagogue. Jesus identified this rejection with His prophetic statement about a prophet's honor.

There is an additional aspect to Jesus' response that must not be overlooked. Mark wrote that Jesus could do no mighty work in Nazareth. Mark recorded that Jesus was surprised at the unbelief of the people (6:6). Jesus never lost the ability to be surprised or astonished at the response or action of people. Even though He knew why the people were unreceptive to Him in Nazareth, He still was surprised. Rejection is an extremely strong and devastating response by one person to another. Even in knowing that we must guard against becoming so cynical, we deny the pain of rejection.

As Jesus cut through rejection at Nazareth, His action pointed toward two practical instructions. After acknowledging and accepting the rejection and the rejectors, it is necessary to get on with the task to which one is committed. The work of discipleship must never depend on the consensus of everyone. Everybody needs and wants praise and recognition; however, the ongoing work of discipleship must never become dependent on the daily shot in the arm in the form of praise. If the praise becomes the motive, then there will be more and more grandstanding and playing to the gallery and less and less ministry being done. The praise for a well-researched, well-crafted, and well-delivered sermon lasts almost as long as it takes to deliver the sermon. Usually, by 12:15 on Sunday afternoon the appreciation and praise for the sermon has abated. I doubt that praise for work in other professions lasts any longer.

We can see clearly, through Mark's account, the obstacle to Jesus' ministry that stubborn prejudice, lack of faith, and closed minds erected. What is appalling is that we do not see the correlation to our own attitudes and approaches to life. How often have we suggested that the approach of reconciliation is fine in the church or has to do with salvation but has nothing to do with the way things are in the real world? Have we not said with our living if not with our voices that peace, justice, brotherhood, and sisterhood are fine in the church; but they just don't work in government, business, or international relations?

An indictment leveled at the church by many who are outside the church is that the church is no different than any other place or organization. My response is *yes* and *no*. Yes, the church is like every other organization. It is made up of people who have a variety of interests, ideas, and attitudes, and who make a variety of mistakes. The result is: there often is conflict in the church. There will be conflict in the church. But the church is not like every other organization because it has an effective model for resolving conflict. The model is Jesus the Christ who sought to reconcile the differences between people and between people and God rather than to fuel the fires of hatred and animosity.

I found Jesse Jackson's approach to international relations refreshing in 1984 when he obtained the release of Lt. Goodman and, later, forty-six prisoners from Cuba. He learned the method of conciliatory negotiations from the Master Reconcilor. Jackson's approach is a signal that the methods of Christ can and do work in the real world. We in the church often have failed to follow the instructions of Jesus within the community of faith to resolve our conflicts. Thus the accusations of those outside the church have been true that the church is no different from any other organization. Until our promise and our performance become more consistent then those outside the church have a legitimate complaint and will find little or no reason to consider becoming a part of it.

Jesus did no mighty work in Nazareth, not because He would not but because He could not. The resistance, rejection, and closed minds of the people kept Him from His mighty works. Here is evidence in Jesus' ministry where the power of God was thwarted by the power of the people. God did a dangerous thing by creating human beings free because they can use their freedom both to reject God and to prevent His love from being effective.

There are at least two additional ways Jesus redemptively responded to rejection. He developed authority, and He established relationships. It was said of Jesus on numerous occasions that He spoke as one having authority. From where did He get it? Certainly it did not come from rabbinic school nor from the carpenter's shop, although His interaction with scribes and Pharisees in the synagogue and Temple were instructive, and His work in the carpenter's shop helped Jesus relate to people. Jesus' authority was not conferred upon Him from some external source. Rather, His authority came from within as He developed His relationship with God. Thus He spoke as one having authority rather than as an authoritarian. One who has authority is secure in that authority and has no need to impose his authority onto another. One who is authoritarian has received his authority outside himself, is insecure with it, and feels compelled to impose his standards and regulations onto others.

As a second redemptive response to rejection, Jesus established relationships. Jesus clearly demonstrated in His life that human beings are relational by nature and by need. Mark recorded that one of the reasons Jesus chose disciples was because of His need for human companionship (Mark 3:14). The significance of companionship is inferred in the event that Mark recorded immediately following the rejection in Nazareth. Jesus took the opportunity to begin sending out His disciples by twos. The disciples were to travel lightly, stop briefly, seek a hearing in every appropriate way; but they were not to force themselves or their message onto anyone. They were to hurry to find people who would be responsive to the message they brought.

Hospitality was regarded as a duty among the Hebrew people. Therefore, it was taken for granted that the disciples would be given food and lodging. If they arrived in a place that was unresponsive to the Word of God, they were to shake the dust off their feet from that place. This was a symbolic act, like a warning. It was not to be hostile or cynical. This instruction was important because the disciples were not to spend time and energy attempting to argue or persuade people. They were to present their message and react according to the response received.

Perhaps the most illustrative example from the Master regarding these instructions was His interaction with the rich ruler. The ruler had kept all of the religious laws from his youth up, and Jesus instructed him to sell what he had and give it to the poor. The young man sorrowfully left Jesus. What did Jesus do? He let him go. What would we do? We would run down the road after him, yelling, "Wait a minute! Stop! Let's talk. I think we can work out a deal."

Calling disciples to be with Him and sending them out by twos was Jesus' way of saying that no one is to go it alone. When a person does try to go it alone, one becomes like the fisherman in *The Old Man and the Sea* who went out too far, and all that he managed to bring back was the huge skeleton of what might have been. One of the causes of burnout in any situation whether it be family life, vocation, or church involvement is trying to go it alone. Even the Lone Ranger needed Tonto. Human beings are not self-made, and we are not self-sufficient.

We are relational creatures by nature and by need. That makes us susceptible to rejection, and it also provides the greatest antidote for rejection, that is relationship with one or more fellow human beings who can be supportive during such experiences. It is those relationships that begin to open the expanses of God's presence to a person's life.

It was during His life and through His relationships that Jesus began to encounter more and more God's presence and care. Was it not this awareness that sustained Him in His greatest time of need? Was it not with God that He related throughout His life, and when life was slipping from Him, was it not upon God whom He called from the cross? It was God who had sustained Him in previous rejections, and it was God who sustained Him through His last and most difficult rejection. He lived out of the promise and died in the promise that God would never leave Him or abandon Him.

You and Rejection

With all these words about rejection in the Bible, what does this have to do with you and me living here and now? What about rejection you have experienced? What is it that is so terrible about rejection? Whatever form rejection takes in a person's life, one feels unloved. To feel unloved is a horrible feeling because it is part of human nature to have the need to love and to be loved. Every human being has the need for the warmth and acceptance of at least one other person. The development of self-worth occurs by feeling and experiencing the worth and value that another person communicates to the individual.

Several years ago an experiment was done with Harlow monkeys, named for the man who designed the experiment. The purpose was to determine if nurture was as necessary as nutriment for the development of infant monkeys. Two groups of monkeys were used. The monkeys in each group were given the same amount and quality of food. The only variable was how the monkeys were fed. One group was fed by their mothers while the other group was fed mechanically through imitation mother monkeys made of wire and fur. The monkeys fed by their natural mothers grew normally while those which did not have the nurture of their mothers developed much more slowly, were thin, and their growth was stunted. These monkeys needed nurture as well as nutriment for healthy development.

Human beings need the positive reinforcement that comes through the care of at least one other person in order to develop self-worth and value. If a person does not receive positive reinforcement then the tendency is to interpret what happens to him as negative reinforcement. There seems to be no neutral ground. Even what may be offered with the intention of being neutral is interpreted by the recipient as negative. Non-committal input is perceived and received as apathy which is the opposite of love. Ernest Campbell told a story that illustrates the point. A nine-year-old girl said in an essay, "I don't know exactly what a family is, but I know one thing—your friends can go off and say they don't want to be your friends any more, but people just can't go off and say they don't want to be your family any more."[3] Isn't this what God intends for us in the Church to be: a family that is open and receptive to all who have been received by God?

Love and acceptance develop in a person because he has been loved and accepted. A person cannot be rejected continually from infancy without feeling that he is worthless and valueless as a human being. In the story of Gary Gilmore, a convicted murder who was later executed, one of the startling factors about his life was the complete absence of anyone who treated him as a person of worth. Even the uncle who gave Gilmore a job and seemed to try to help him get established had nothing kind to say to him. The uncle often used derogatory language and called him stupid and dumb whenever Gary did anything the uncle did not like. The distinction between love and unlove seems to be the conscious or unsconscious purpose in mind of the lover or the nonlover.[4] Love or unlove is a circular process that expands and enlarges in the direction that it begins. It is nearly impossible for a person to believe and experience the love of God if one has not experienced the love of at least one human being. If one has not been loved by somebody, one will have difficulty knowing what love is and trusting what it means to be loved.

To experience love and to be able to love requires courage and involves risk. To venture out in life, to grow in any dimension is to experience pain as well as joy. The more lovingly a person lives, the more risks he will take. It is the security usually of parents' love, reflected in a person's self-love, which enables that person to risk the unknown. Rejection is part of the risk. The irony is that those who have experienced and felt the most love and acceptance are able to take the most risks of rejection and experience the least rejection while those who have received the least or no love take less risks of being rejected but experience rejection the most often. Part of the latter's common approach is: "I'll reject you before you reject me." This becomes a self-fulfilling prophecy.

Being a disciple of Christ involves the risk of being rejected. However, long before rejection is possible, the disciple has ample opportunity to be accepted and loved. Jesus did not call His disciples and immediately throw them to the world. He called them to be with Him first. Jesus established relationships with them because He and they needed a common bond. When Jesus did send out His disciples, He sent them out in twos. Their relationship to one another provided support and encouragement for the tasks ahead of them. In addition, Jesus was continually instructing His disciples about what they might expect and anticipate in their work. At times Jesus seemed to be bending over backwards to inform His disciples what was involved for one who followed Him. Rejection was a real possibility, but they would be able to face that because of their relationship with Him and with each other.

A major task of contemporary disciples of Christ is to find and experience nurture for their lives. A primary function of the church is its worship of God which serves as the feeding time and place for disciples of Christ. Having a support group that helps nurture a

88 Redemptive Responses of Jesus

person then enables the person to take risks in ministering to others, risks of being rejected. Being a human being makes one vulnerable to being rejected. Discovering and experiencing God's love and acceptance is the antidote for rejection. John stated it well, "We love, because he first loved us" (1 John 4:19). We can see in the life and ministry of Jesus how intensely He loved and how strongly He was rejected. There is a correlation between His being loved, being able to love, and His being able to respond redemptively to rejection. Even at the end of His life when rejection of Him was the most intense, Jesus seemed the most intent on loving. He refused to reject those who rejected Him. He had no need for such a response because all along He had been making redemptive responses to rejection by acknowledging and accepting His rejectors. Love is a powerful force of will and intention that gives a person the courage to translate will into action. Love enables a person to move out into the unknown and into the future against resistance that is generated by fear. Rejection is the response of a person who is frightened and threatened. May the life and ministry of Jesus serve as impetus to guide His disciples in responding redemptively to rejection.

Notes

1. Ernest Campbell. *Locked in a Room with Open Doors.* (Waco: Word Books, Inc., 1974), p. 13.
2. Frederick Buechner. *Wishful Thinking: A Theological ABC.* (San Francisco: Harper and Row), 1975, p. 20.
3. Campbell, *Locked in a Room with Open Doors,* p. 18.
4. Scott M. Peck. *The Road Less Traveled: A New Psychology of Love, Traditional and Spiritual Growth.* (New York: Simon and Schuster, 1978), p. 89.

5
Responding to Charlantry

Matthew 21: 12-17

When you think of Jesus getting angry, what incident comes to mind? Do you recall the story of Jesus chasing the merchants and the money changers from the Temple? I suspect this is the event that most people think of when they consider Jesus being angry. Of course, there were other times when Jesus got angry. Throughout this book I have pointed many of them out. Then I have shown how He used His anger to respond redemptively to the people with whom He was angry.

Many have read the accounts of Jesus cleansing the Temple while wearing blinders and ear plugs. Having come to the Scripture with a preconceived idea of what Jesus was like, many have struggled to incorporate this picture of Jesus into the image they already had.

In this particular event during Jesus' ministry, not only did He speak, but He also acted. Actually, He acted, and then He spoke. The Gospel writers had different sources for their information about Jesus, yet all four writers include this incident in their accounts. Apparently, what Jesus did was as startling to His disciples and those in the Temple as it has been to the generations who have read about it. John suggested that the disciples were so startled that they had to think of a Scripture passage to support the action of Jesus (2:17).

Jesus Cleansed the Temple

Although all of the Gospels tell about Jesus' cleansing of the Temple, there are variations in their accounts. John placed this event at the beginning of Jesus' ministry while the Synoptics put it at the end of Jesus' ministry, on the day of His triumphal entry into Jerusalem. Matthew was the most verbose of the Synoptics while Luke gave the least amount of ink to this event. For comparison, Mark used sixty words to tell about this incident while Luke used twenty-five.[1]

The Temple complex in Jerusalem contained thirteen acres. It was made up of courts within courts. The outer court was known as the Court of the Gentiles, and anyone was permitted in that area. This was where the merchants and money changers were. It was here that Jesus made a whip of cords (John 2:15), drove out the sheep and oxen, poured out the coins of the money changers, turned over the tables, and accused those who were selling pigeons that they had turned His Father's house into a marketplace (John 2:16). It must have been a bizarre scene. The whip of cords probably was made of branches or stalks like the type that would have been used for bedding. No one was permitted to bring sticks or weapons into the Temple, so the whip would not have been a strip of leather or a stick. Jesus herded the animals out and may have stung them with His handcrafted switch. He stung the merchants with the words, "Take these things away" (John 2:16).

Jesus' was protesting abuses of the Temple. He was not against the helpful practices that had developed to assist the worshipers. Jews were expected to come to the Temple for at least one of the three major festivals each year. Passover was by far the most popular of the three. Many of them traveled great distances from their homes to Jerusalem. This made it impractical, if not impossible, to bring their animal sacrifices with them. For a long time before Jesus lived, there had been merchants who sold sacrificial animals at the Temple. There also was the Temple tax which had to be paid by each worshiper. This tax amounted to approximately eight cents. A day's wages in that time was about nine cents. The Temple tax provided about $125,000 annually to the Temple which was used for the maintenance of the Temple and to provide the livelihood for the priests.[2] The Temple tax had to be paid with clean money. Money that had the inscription of a king was considered unclean because the imprint of the king was identified as a graven image. This was the reason for money changers in the Temple.

There were merchants in Jerusalem who probably sold sacrifical animals at cheaper prices than those sold in the court of the Gentiles. Of course the animals had to pass inspection. Since the high priest received a percentage of the receipts of the animals sold in the Temple area, it may have been difficult to find an animal anywhere other than in the court of the Gentiles that would pass inspection. Initially, the selling of the sacrifical animals on the Temple grounds had served the needs of the worshipers. Jesus was not opposed to that.

Jesus' anger was directed at the merchants and money changers because they were exploiting people in the name of religion. When people are being exploited, they become angry and argumentative. Is it not possible that there was so much haggling over the prices being charged that the atmosphere was thick with hostility? The court of the Gentiles was in such a state of confusion that prayer and preparation for worship were nearly impossible. Jesus did not interrupt a worship service. Rather, he cleared an area where worship could occur. The court of the Gentiles was the one area reserved for response to God by all races. Jesus repudiated in principle an establishment where trade had usurped the place of worship, and sacrifice had become a substitute for worldwide compassion.

Luke suggested that after cleansing the Temple Jesus taught there everyday. The result was that the people listened to Him, and the religious leaders plotted to kill Him (19:48). Mark wrote that the religious leaders were so irate with Jesus that they plotted to kill Him, but they were hesitant to take action because of the popularity Jesus experienced from the crowd (11:18). Matthew recorded that after Jesus turned the tables on the merchants and the money-changers, the lame and the blind came to Him and He healed them. Why did they come after this event? I wonder if they had been exploited by some of these dealers because of their handicaps. Now they had an advocate for their situations and concerns. Jesus healed them.

How was this received? The chief priests and lawyers were *outraged* by the wonderful things Jesus had done! Wasn't that an unusual response to the help and healing that Jesus brought? Of course, the lawyers and the chief priests were still smarting from the cut in revenue which Jesus had caused by the wild scene a brief time earlier. One thing that will anger people quickly is to do something that reduces their income. Jesus had done just that.

Not only did the blind and the lame come to Him for help and healing, but the children were shouting in the Temple. Nothing is more irritating to people who are angry and upset than to see a bunch of children who are happy and enjoying themselves. Children just don't seem to see the seriousness of life! I have learned to trust the instincts, insights, and perceptions of children. If a child thinks that a person is good, in all likelihood the person is good. George Macdonald said that he placed no value in the alleged Christianity of a man at whose door or garden gate children were afraid to play.[3]

What the children were shouting was as disturbing to the religious leaders as was the fact that they were shouting. The children were shouting, "Hosanna to the Son of David." Earlier in the day when Jesus rode into Jerusalem, the crowd had shouted the same thing. No doubt some of the children had been there. Now they recognized Him in the Temple. Not only had they seen His deeds of kindness to the blind and the lame, but also such kindness was characteristic of the long-awaited Messiah. Jesus' action toward those in need helped reveal His nature to the children who looked and listened with open eyes and ears.

The religious leaders revealed how threatened they were with the question they asked Jesus, "Do you hear what these are saying?" (Matt. 21:16). This question had a condescending tone to it. Only if Jesus were deaf would He be unable to hear what the children were saying. Of course, the fact that He heard what they said and did not refute them was self-incriminating as far as the religious leaders were concerned. Part of what was threatening to the religious leaders was the implication made by the praise of the children, "Hosanna to the Son of David!" (v. 15). *Hosanna* originally was a Hebraic invocation addressed to God that meant "O save!" Although it later became an expression of joyous acclamation, hosanna continued to have the plea for salvation wrapped in it. Who was Jesus to allow the inference that He would bring salvation? From what would He save people? He had just saved many of them from the abuses and charlatanry of merchants and money changers who were a part of the religious establishment.

What Jesus had done was to ask the people to throw off the traditional structures that had been accumulating for a thousand years. Jesus was disruptive in the Temple when, through the cleansing of the Temple, He called the very heart of Judaism to radical renewal. Jesus' approach sent the religious leaders rocking and reeling because in turning over the tables He was turning the tables on them to demonstrate the abuse that was being done in the name of religion. That is why He quoted Jeremiah (7:11) when He said they had made the Temple a den of thieves. Surely, His reference was to their overcharging for goods and services that the people needed and wanted to use in their worship of God. Jesus also quoted from Isaiah (56:7) when he said, "My house shall be called a house of prayer." Jesus was clearing a way so people could pray. Then in response to the question the religious leaders had about what the children were saying, Jesus again referred to Scripture (Ps. 118:25-26) to support both what the children said and His response.

Jesus outscriptured the scripturalists in His responses to their questions and concerns. The result was that they became so enraged that they plotted to kill Him. Until this time, His chief enemies had been the Pharisees. The Pharisees and the Sadducees were bitter theological enemies. However, they became cohorts against Jesus, their common enemy. The scene that Jesus created in the Temple sealed His fate. It was the event that solidified the Pharisees and the Sadducees to work toward a common objective. Perhaps because of who Jesus was, the way He conducted His ministry, and who the Pharisees and Sadducees were, it was inevitable that they eventually would kill Jesus. Maybe that was the only secure thing the religious leaders knew to do. Nevertheless, Jesus' action in the Temple so agitated and angered the religious leadership that then they began planning together to destroy Him. Nothing fuels a cause more intensely than a holy cause. When the Pharisees and Sadducees concluded that to destroy Jesus was the right thing to do religiously, their motivation became unstoppable.

John had a different ending to this incident in the Temple. Of course, by placing the event at the beginning of Jesus' ministry, John did not suggest that the incident sealed Jesus' fate with the religious leadership. First, according to John, Jesus' disciples scurried to find a defense for Jesus' action in chasing animals and people from the Temple. Somebody went thumbing through the Scripture until a finger fell on Psalm 69:9. Then they had justification for Jesus' bizaare action, "Zeal for thy house has consumed me." The word *consume* had a double-edged meaning. It referred to the intensity of zeal from within and to the hostility that zeal could provoke from without. The purpose of worship was and is to cultivate a consuming zeal for God Himself. This was Jesus' intention, and His intention challenged and confronted the religious leaders because their zeal to worship God had been tainted by their profit margin.

Naturally, the religious leaders wanted a sign to convince them that Jesus' action in the Temple had been justified. I say naturally because, when people have made up their minds already, they tend to taunt people to convince them, knowing full well that whatever sign is given they will be able to offer another explanation of what the sign means. Nevertheless, Jesus suggested a sign to them. He said that they could destroy this temple, and in three days He would raise it up. That sailed right over their heads, and they began talking about the great building program they had underway.

I never cease to be amazed at conversations in church. What receives the most popular response so often is not work done with human relationships but construction and maintenance work on the building. This was true in this situation with Jesus. The Jewish leaders scoffed at Jesus for suggesting a three-day reconstruction job when it had taken forty-six years to get the Temple in the shape it was in, and another forty was expected before the job would be completed. Of course Jesus' reference was to His body as "this temple," but His audience misunderstood. Why did they misunderstand? Was it because of the context of the conversation? Surely Jesus gestured to His body when He made His statement. It was not His nature to make statements to confuse or cause misunderstanding. Of course, people can hear most anything. It seems they especially hear what they want to hear in church. Maybe the same was true of these religious leaders in their conversation with Jesus. Already they were angry with Jesus. I have noticed that when my anger is raging against someone I miss some of the things the person says to me and some of the gestures made. Maybe it was so in this case for Jesus.

Jesus' action in the Temple was in line with the Hebrew prophetic tradition. Often the prophets acted out their message. The more senses they caused their audience to use in receiving the message, the better were the chances that the message would hit home. Jeremiah smashed a clay pot to illustrate what would happen if Israel didn't shape up. Hosea named his children some truly awful names, so everytime anybody called out their names they were reminded of their father's prophecy. Jesus acted out His message. By His action Jesus reclaimed the Temple for its rightful purpose and use. Later His action was used as evidence of His destructive nature and why He ought to be destroyed. At His trial Jesus was separated from the people so that His popularity could not work in His favor and save His life as it had done in the Temple. "The chief priests and the scribes and the principal men of the people sought to destroy him; but they did not find anything they could do, for all the people hung upon his words" (Luke 19:47-48).

Nothing angered Jesus more than to see people exploiting their fellow human beings. When Jesus cleansed the Temple, He leveled His anger at those who blocked the way of worship for others. Here were religious leaders who were exploiting their fellow human beings and baptizing their actions in religious language. On the basis of providing sacrifices without blemish and coins without graven images, they were extorting their fellow human beings. They were huckstering piety for profit. Jesus was angered by it, and He used His anger to motivate Him to healthy action. He confronted those who were wrong, and He sought to help those who were in need. Jesus' anger was not a negative berating of character; rather, He forced the exploiters and extortioners to stop sinning against their fellow human beings at least for that day. He also sought to clear a place for people to engage in authentic worship.

Contemporary Charlatanry

No profession is exempt from those who abuse and misuse their position and authority for personal advantage. Most professions have some means of redress if a person has just cause to demonstrate that a breach of professional responsibility has occurred. The legal profession has its bar association and the American Medical Association serves in a similar fashion for the medical profession. One who has been offended also may take his case to court.

Religious exploitation and extortion did not end in the Temple on the first Palm Sunday. These sins have continued through the centuries, and there is evidence of them today. Professional ministers have no organization that develops a standard of excellence or set of principles by which a clergy person is to abide. We react with horror at such a suggestion. If anyone should abide by an ethical standard, surely the clergy would, and surely they would know what the standard ought to be! I really do not need to argue the point. I suspect you can think of at least one person in a position of religious leadership who through extortion, exploitation, or manipulation has abused the confidence entrusted to him or her by the people. Some religious charlatans have come to national and international attention. Jim Jones is a recent example. Others have gone unnoticed except by the people they have conned.

I suspect there has been an increase in religious exploitation and extortion in the past decade because there has been an increase in interest in religion in our time. Our culture is in a time of transition. We are moving out of the industrial age and into the informational age. History is replete with evidence that revival of religion parallels cultural transitions. During times of great change, turmoil, and flux, people desire structure. They often look for it in religion. I have several friends who were pastors in Washington, DC, during World War II. They often comment about the overflow crowds they had for worship services during those bleak days. The analysis of that situation is that when the whole world was in such a state of turmoil as it was in the 1940s, people sought security in religion. However, after the turmoil passed, people became more secure, and their need for religion was reduced. Now those same churches in Washington, DC, are never filled for worship services, yet there are many more people in metropolitan Washington now than there were forty years ago.

The revival of religion in our land is not showing in our churches. None of the mainline denominations are showing any great influx of members. While some very fundamentalist congregations are showing great statistical growth, much of the growth is coming from people who are crossing denominational lines rather than from people becoming involved in church for the first time.

During the past decade when culture has been in flux and interest in religion has been on the rise, the electronic church has developed. With its development, the possibility has increased for charlatanry. There has been a rising desire and search for celebrityhood enhanced by the lure of the spotlight. The church often has been confronted by the temptation to use the world's yardstick to measure its effectivness. That yardstick tends to suggest that bigger is better and to offer the corporate model as a role model. The electronic church encourages this approach with the lure of the spotlight. Desire for and being in the spotlight makes it difficult to see or distinguish who others are. The spotlight tends to make the one standing in it seem bigger than life. How the world spells success and how Christ spells success are at least a world apart.

What the electronic church has done is to reinforce the existing religious beliefs of its viewers. The electronic church has not been an effective tool of evangelism, bringing good news to those who have not heard it. Another aspect of televised religious programming is the request for money, a recent study indicates. The most prominent electronic church ministries have been the ones most likely to request money, and their requests have been numerous. Four out of ten programs included three or more requests during the course of each telecast. The average minimum request was for thirty-one dollars, and the average maximum request was for six-hundred dollars.[4] Much of the money is asked for selfish reasons, most often to keep the programs on the air.

One example of religious huckstering that disturbed me was when the preacher, early in his television broadcast, urged his viewers to send him twenty-five-hundred dollars to purchase an acre of mountain property. Later in the broadcast the sales pitch intensified as the viewers were told that if they could not or would not buy an acre, half acres were available for half that price. Even later, a third appeal was made for people to purchase one quarter of an acre for one fourth that amount. If people would send in the money, they would each receive a copy of a deed for a portion of the mountain. The individual would own a piece of the mountain, but the property would remain under the control and use of the TV minister and/or his congregation.

Part of the deceptiveness of much religious programming is the image projected. The subliminal message is that if we do what is suggested by these primetime preachers, we will be successful in life like they and their program guests. Practically invisible on these programs are blue-collar workers, the unemployed, the retired, and housewives.[5] Religious programming is popular because it confirms what people already believe. It helps them feel secure, and through this security it lures them to contribute money to keep life as it is on television. Secular television, however, is what really challenges people's beliefs, their church attendance, and giving.[6] What the church needs to be doing is teaching people about television and how to deal with it, so they can control television rather than it controlling them.

Some of the religious huckstering that occurs comes through the electronic church because people are being controlled by it. That is exploitation and extortion baptized in the language of Zion.

One of the issues which many electronic-church preachers seek to meet is security. Often what they suggest will provide security resembles the world's standard of success rather than that of Jesus. A portion of a poem by David Steele about Moses speaks to this issue. Moses is in conversation with God.

> "But," continues Moses, "I can't
> Go 'round talking about you very well.
> I don't even know your name."
> Now there's a kicker here
> As both Moses and Yahweh know.
> Moses is a Hebrew.
> And names mean something special.
> Those Hebrews feel that if you know someone's name
> Then you have a handle on that person.
> You know them in an intimate way.
> You can predict and control their actions.
> What Moses is looking for here
> Is the kind of thing those TV preachers
> Have down pat.
>
> You know what I mean.
> You flip the channels and those preachers
> Know just about everything there is to know
> About God.
> They know just what God wants everybody to believe:
> And how God wants us to vote . . .
> And where to send our money . . .
> And who we're supposed to love . . .
> And who we're supposed to hate . . .
> And when the world is going to end . . .
> (Within 15 minutes or so).
> It's impressive . . . what those preachers know about God.
> You get the feeling that God

Checks in with them each morning
For marching orders.[7]

Such an approach and attitude as this is a form of charlatanry. Charlatanry is a form of the word *charlatan* that comes from the Italian *ciarlatano,* which means babbler, idle talker. Charlatan is applied to any person who pretends to have knowledge or ability that he does not have. A charlatan is an impostor. The selling of indulgences during the Middle Ages is one of the more infamous acts of charlatanry in the life of the church. Martin Luther's reaction against this practice was a major contributing factor in the Protestant Reformation.

The local congregation is not exempt from charlatanry. It may be as subtle as someone encouraging a prospective member to join by saying, "This congregation can really use you." Too many members have been used by the congregation for the benefit of the congregation, and when they were of no more use, then the congregation had no further interest in them. Haven't you seen examples where an excellent teacher finally burned out, or where a capable leader kept being asked to do more and more? Finally, the person dropped out of the church. Maybe it was the only way one could deal with having been abused by the church.

The more common form of charlatanry in the local congregation is that of a religious leader who manipulates members or the entire congregation for personal gain. There are a number of payoffs that come from the game of charlatanry. The payoff of extortion is money. Generally, extortion in the church takes place when a minister milks a congregation for all kinds of financial rewards through a variety of shenanigans. However, the other side of this issue is a member or members of the congregation who seek to control and maneuver the congregation the direction they want it to go by designating their money to particular projects or by withholding their contributions with the hopes of shutting down the effectiveness of the congregation.

Once that is accomplished, then they hope to persuade the membership to do things their way.

Sometime after I left one of my former pastorates, one family left the church because they did not feel they were having enough influence in the congregation. The woman stated, "Without our financial support the church will fold in six months. Then we will come back, reopen it, and name it Jones Chapel." (You can guess what the family name was!) This was charlatanry because it imposed the will and direction of a few on all. The primary purpose for the church's existence is to worship God. When the power plays of charlantry are occurring, many people are being kept from worshiping God. Jesus had very stern words and action for such religious leaders in the Temple. In addition to money and control, other payoffs for religious quackery include power, prestige, popularity, manipulative, and exploitative abilities. What is wrong with these payoffs is that they turn people into objects to be used by one or more people for personal gain or benefit.

Charlatanry involves some of the craftiness of a con artist. You really haven't lived until you have been conned. I suspect that each of us has been conned at least once. The question that arises is: how can we diagnose charlatanry before we have been used and abused.

Diagnosing Charlatanry

Here are four things which can help diagnose charlatanry. No doubt you can think of others to add. I would like your input. The longer our lists, the quicker we will be able to spot chalatanry as it approaches. One of the first signs of charlatanry is an invitation, an encouragement, or even a requirement that persons sacrifice their intellect. This was the devil's approach to Jesus in the wilderness temptations. The devil told Jesus that if He would just fall down and worship him, turn all thinking over to him, and let him make all of the decisions, he would give Jesus all the kingdoms of the world. In many of the science/religion debates of the decades, often those within the church have asked people to sacrifice their intellect when it came to questions of science. If there was a conflict between faith and reason, reason had to go. That was easier than examining with reason what their faith meant and had to say at a point of conflict.

A subtle example of this happened during my high school days. It came from my pastor during a Sunday morning sermon. I don't think it was his intention to ask us to sacrifice our intellects, but in effect that was what he did with this illustration. He told about two of the young people who had gone from the congregation to a nearby state university. In biology class they were being taught about the theory of evolution. They had reported this to the pastor. The way they had chosen to protest this teaching, since it was against their belief system, was to refuse to answer the test questions that related to evolution. These two students and their decisions were held up to the congregation through a sermon illustration as examples for the rest of us to follow.

This was a subtle invitation for us to sacrifice our intellects rather than to seek to develop them to the best of our abilities as part of our stewardship responsibilities. Charlatanry encourages the sacrifice of intellect because those who turn over their thinking to another become dependent upon those who do their thinking for them. Such an approach is an easier life, but a deadly one. Jonestown, Guyana, is the most grotesque example in recent memory.

A second clue to charlatanry is authoritarianism. Authority comes from within and works its way out into the involvements and relationships a person has. Authoritarianism is an external imposition of one person's will, opinion, or ideas upon others. Authoritarianism may result from someone wanting and needing very much to be in control and/or from insecurity about oneself. There may be other reasons, but it is not unusual for one who responds in an authoritarian manner to do so because he is pretending to have knowledge or ability that he does not. One of his key phrases may be, "Just trust me." Richard Nixon made that phrase popular and then infamous in 1973. The authoritarian person lacks humility and is closed toward any instruction from others.

On several occasions during his ministry, Jesus was referred to as One who spoke or acted with authority. His authority came from within. He never sought to impose His authority or will on anyone. He was forever leaving people room to choose for themselves. There was always space for people to make up their own minds, rather than having a decision imposed on them.

A third sign of charlatanry is the encouragement to live in the past. The best has already been, and our only hope is to try to get life back to the way it used to be. The view is that life was perfect in the good old days. This strong nudge into nostalgia is prevalent today with the attacks on public education and the solution being offered is to have prayer in the classroom. It is suggested that God currently is absent but can be carted into the classroom with a government-written, government-sponsored prayer addressed "To Whom It May Concern." Of course God is wherever Christians are, even in the classroom. Religious leaders bemoan the good old days when people were not faced with the problems, stress, and issues they have to face now, the days when more people attended church, and the days when life was simpler.

Those days were when they were much younger, more energetic, and more optimistic. They fail to realize that the older people then were bemoaning the development of the automobile, ankle-high dresses, and ducktail hair styles. The move to live nostalgically is a move to avoid or escape reality. It is contrary to biblical faith which undauntedly affirms that the best is yet to be rather than that the best already has been.

Charlatanry also is reflected in an excessive desire for or promise of security. There always is the clamor in our lives to stay the course. The status quo is so desirable because we already are familiar with it. Even when the need and benefits of change can be clearly seen, the lure of security that comes with staying the course is so enticing.

Don't rock the boat was the instruction that many congregations gave to clergy in the 1960s as they sought to confront and challenge racism in and out of the church. A similar safe approach is en-

couraged and taken by many today with regard to sexism and the
leadership roles of women in the church. One woman said to me,
"Wouldn't it bother you if half of the deacons in your church were
women?" I responded, "No. As a matter-of-fact, this year half of our
deacons will be women." With astonishment she responded, "And
that doesn't bother you?" "No," I assured her. Well, I don't really
think I assured her. I think the whole idea was unsettling and frightening to her.

Biblical Charlatans

The Bible has several examples of charlatans. Three that stand out
to me are Saul, Ananias, and Sapphira. Saul was the first king of Israel
and he had a very difficult task. He had to help the nation make the
transition from the time of the judges into the monarchy. Saul became
threatened by the popularity of David, and he lost the support of
Samuel. As a result Saul was given over to ecstatic experiences which
sometimes rendered him incapable of governing. Saul became extremely authoritarian and saw the laws as good for the people but
exempted himself from obeying all of them, such as the use of a
medium to contact someone who was dead (1 Sam. 28:3-17). Later,
out of his distress, Saul would not eat. Eventually, when a battle went
against him, Saul killed himself. He was a vocational failure.

What seems to have happened to Saul is that he invested all of his
energy into performing his task as king and religious leader of Israel.
He really developed an idolatry of his role as leader. As a result, Saul
resorted to magic and superstition as a means of cunning to maintain
and secure his position as king and religious leader. Saul was a power-
oriented religious leader who seemed to be more intent on being great
than being good. He was plagued by incompetence, inadequacy, and
fears of personal weakness.

Two other charlatans in the Bible were Ananias and Sapphira. They
were a husband-and-wife team mentioned in Acts 5 who were involved in the early church. Their desire to be popular and to have
some power and authority in the church seemed to have been their

motives for pretending to do something they didn't. At a time when the church was in great financial difficulty, Barnabas sold a piece of property and gave all of the proceeds to the church (4:36-37). The church probably responded with excited enthusiasm and poured all kinds of accolades onto Barnabas. Ananais and Sapphira seemed to have observed this and decided to do the same thing, with a minor exception. They decided to keep part of the proceeds but to tell the church they had given all they had received for the property to the church. Now it was not expected or required that they sell their property, nor were they required to give all of the proceeds to the church. However, this was their act of charlatanry to influence and control the church. Each made the claim to the church of the generosity of the gift, and each fell dead when confronted with the truth which the church leaders had discovered.

Ways to Respond Redemptively to Charlatanry

Charlatanry is both ancient and modern. Nothing angered Jesus more than to see extortion and exploitation baptized in religious language. He responded to charlatanry with both words and deeds. His approach can be instructive. First, Jesus cleared a way for people to worship God. The worship of God is primary, and nothing should keep people from that. Jesus also embraced ambiguity. He was not opposed to people making sacrifices in the Temple. He did not oppose sacrifices being available for purchase there. He was angered that the convenience of the sacrificial animals had become a requirement, so the merchants had captive customers. He was angered that people were using religion for commercial exploitation. Thus He embraced the ambiguity of supporting the Temple practices but not to the extent of extortion.

Often what charlatanry offers us today is clear-cut either/or options. The issues of life are not that clearly defined. We have to embrace ambiguity like the man who said, "[Lord] I believe; help my unbelief!" (Mark 9:24). Abraham embraced ambiguity in his faith commitment when he left Ur. He went out not knowing where he was going, but knowing with whom he was going.

A third redemptive response to charlatanry is seeking to help relieve people of guilt they feel for their own well-being, but not for someone else's benefit. Religion continues because of the felt need of people to deal with guilt. This need keeps religion popular, and being popular always leaves religion open to racketeering, profiteering, and fraud.

Responding redemptively to charlatanry is also done by allowing ourselves to be vulnerable to fear, pain, and suffering. This was Jesus' approach in the Temple. He knew the climate well enough to know that to take the action He took against the merchants and the money changers would put Him in a life-threatening situation. But He had to take a stand on the side of the oppressed, the victims of extortion and exploitation, regardless of the pain and suffering that He might have to face. Therein is the risk for us if we stand with the oppressed and against the charlatans. Here is where we need to stand. We should be able to do nothing else.

Notes

1. Malcolm O. Tolbert, "Luke," *The Broadman Bible Commentary* (Nashville: Broadman Press, 1969), vol. 9, p. 152.

2. William Barclay, *The Mind of Jesus* (New York: Harper Brothers, 1960), p. 187.

3. William Barclay, *The Gospel of Matthew: The Daily Study Bible Series.* (Philadelphia: The Westminster Press, 1956), vol. 2, p. 275.

4. William F. Fore. "Religion and Television: Report on the Research," *The Christian Century.* vol. 101, no. 23, 18-25 July 1984, p. 711.

5. Ibid., p. 711.

6. Ibid., p. 713.

7. David Steele, "Moses Gets The Nod, Then Exits," *Theology Today,* Oct. 1984, vol. XLI, no. 3, p. 253. Used by permission.

6
Responding to Denial

Matthew 26: 69-75

Denial is one of the basic coping mechanisms people have. We use denial to protect ourselves from the intense pain that comes from a threat to either our existence or our self-esteem. Denial functions as a buffer after unexpected shocking news has come. The period of denial allows someone to collect himself. Usually, after a period of time during which one adjusts to the news, the individual is able to face the reality which he has been denying.

Much has been said and written about denial in recent years, especially as it relates to people who are terminally ill. There are other deaths which we must face and experience before we face our physical death. Jesus suggested that we have to die to ourselves. Have you not been confronted with the death of who you dreamed you were? What person has not arrived at mid-life and come up against the fact that she could not accomplish all of the things she had imagined in life? One of the forms that denial takes for many of us is claiming to be better than we are or promising to deliver with our lives more than we ever do.

This is the classic form of denial that is spoken of so vividly in the Gospels. Peter is the person with whom we immediately associate denial. Peter's experience in the courtyard of the high priest on the night of Jesus' trial is the illustration often held up to demonstrate what denial is and what it does. I will examine this part of Peter's experience. But before I look closely at that chapter in Peter's life, I want to explore other parts of Peter's life because I think there were other times when Peter practiced denial. The courtyard scene is just more blatant. In each of these denial scenes there is evidence that Jesus responded redemptively to the denial in an attempt to reach Peter and to bring to life the person that Jesus saw inside.

Several years ago a theory was put forth in the business world that became known as the Peter Principle. Its formulation was the result of people resisting accountability. When there was a problem in an office or a division with personal irresponsibility, the irresponsible person would be promoted out of the office or division rather than confronted about it. This concept is named for Laurence J. Peter, who first made the observation that people often are promoted to their highest level of *incompetence.*

The First Peter Principle

The first Peter Principle was developed centuries earlier. It is in marked contrast to the approach mentioned above. The first Peter Principle was developed by Jesus through His relationship with Simon Peter. At every turn in that relationship Jesus called Peter to accountability. Examination of Peter's encounters with Jesus will lead us to self-examination which probably will be painful but needful and helpful. It was painful and helpful for Peter. Why should it be different for us? Let us explore the life of Peter as he was involved with Jesus.

Andrew and Simon were brothers. They were fishermen by trade and apparently were in business with James and John. Whenever Simon and Andrew are mentioned together, Simon is mentioned first, and that has contributed to speculation that Simon was the older of the two. There are some differences in the biblical accounts of Jesus' invitation to Simon and Andrew to become His followers. The Synoptics all agree. All three Gospels state that Simon and Andrew were at their boats when Jesus called them. John's Gospel says that Andrew first met Jesus. Then he went to get his brother and told Simon that he had found the Messiah. The four Gospels are in agreement that Simon and Andrew were the first two disciples that Jesus called, and their fishing buddies and partners, James and John, were close behind them.

Few other facts are known about Simon. His father's name was John or Jonah depending upon which Gospel you read. Which John or who Jonah was is unclear. Simon overshadowed his brother, Andrew, who is virtually unknown and hardly ever mentioned other than with Simon. Some evidence indicates that Beth-saida was their hometown, and they operated their fishing business out of Capernaum. Both cities were on the Sea of Galilee. Simon was married. He, his wife, and Andrew apparently lived with Simon's mother-in-law (Mark 1:29-30). It was she that Jesus healed of a fever. Paul wrote that Simon took his wife with him on journeys to various churches (1 Cor. 9:5).

From the time that Jesus extended the invitation onward, Simon was a full-time disciple. A full-time disciple was one who continued his personal association with the teacher as an integral part of the learning process. Simon continued to earn his livelihood as a fisherman. On more than one occasion his boat was used for the disciples to move across the Sea of Galilee. On at least one occasion, his boat was Jesus' pulpit when He spoke to large crowds by the sea. Simon's name appears first in the list of the apostles because he became their spokesman and because he became the respected leader of the church in the first fifteen years of its life as reported in Acts 1—12. The first of the Gospels was written thirty years after the life of Christ. By that time Peter's significant leadership had been well received.

The New Testament uses four names to refer to Simon. Simon, which means flittering dove,[1] is used more often than his Hebrew name, Symeon, which is found in Acts and 2 Peter 1:1. John's Gospel uses the compound name: Simon Peter. Of course, Peter is the dominant name in New Testament usage and the one used most often within the church to refer to him. Simon was his earlier name, and Peter was given to him later. John stated that he was given the name Peter at the time of his call to discipleship. The other Gospel writers indicated that it was sometime later that Jesus identified him as Cephas, Aramaic for Peter, which is Greek for rock. How *flittering dove* became *solid rock* is a moving study of Peter's involvement with Jesus. I suspect that as we explore the changing of Simon into Peter we will see how our stories intersect with his.

One word describes Peter as portrayed in the Gospels: *impetuous.* There are numerous examples of Peter leaping before he looked, speaking before he thought, and answering with what he hoped was the right answer. Jesus became an important authority figure in Peter's life. He wanted desperately to please Jesus and receive His approval. There is an aspect of this desire that comes through in Peter's eagerness to respond to Jesus with quick answers. Sometimes he seemed to want to be the first to speak, to gain recognition. When Jesus was walking on the water, Peter put Jesus to the test to convince the disciples of His identity. What was the test? Jesus commanded Peter to walk on the water toward Him. Matthew, Mark, and John recorded the incident, but only Matthew had Peter walking on the water. Peter always wanted to do whatever Jesus was doing. On another occasion when Jesus said that where He was going the disciples could not go, Peter wanted to know where Jesus was going and why he couldn't go also (John 13:37).

The Great Confession

Peter was with Jesus from the early days of His ministry. He saw Jesus' popularity grow, and he saw the conflict arise between Jesus and the religious leaders. There was a lot of talk about who Jesus was and who He was not. One day Jesus brought up the subject Himself with His disciples. He asked them straightforwardly, "What are you hearing? Who are people saying that I am?" (AP). They gave their answers, "Elijah, Jeremiah, John the Baptist." Then Jesus asked a thorny, pointed question, "But who do *you* say that I am?" The silence was deafening. Somehow they had never thought He would asked them that, or they never thought they would have to answer. But that is the question everyone has to answer about Jesus—Who do *you* say that He is?

The disciples were nervous, uncomfortable. John shifted his weight from one foot to the other. James looked at Andrew, and Andrew looked at Simon. Already they were coming to depend on "old flittering dove" to fill the void caused by silence. They were eager for him to speak, even if he were wrong. Somehow that was better than silence. They preferred to keep quiet and have Jesus think they were ignorant than to open their mouths and remove all doubt. Besides they could count on Simon to blurt out something. This time was no exception. Simon blurted out, "You are the Christ, the Son of the living God" (Matt. 16:16).

Even as impetuous as Simon was, it took a lot of courage to make such a statement. If what he said were true, it could blow the lid off everything. If it were not true, then Simon and the rest of them could get their own lids blown off as blasphemers for thinking such a thing, much less saying it. Jesus responded by giving Simon has very own beatitude, "Blessed are you, Simon Bar-Jona! [which seemed to be what He called him when He really meant business] For flesh and blood has not revealed this to you, but my Father who is in heaven" (Matt. 16:17).

Then Jesus told Simon He was going to give him another name, Peter, which meant *rock*. It would have made more sense to have called Simon "Rocky" in the sense of shaky because that was more descriptive of what Simon had been like. He was forever vacillating, always eager to speak, but seldom if ever eager to listen. He was shaking right then because he had been nervous with all the silence. Then when Jesus blessed him, that made him shake even more. Simon felt his heart jump and his legs melt. He was rocky but no rock.

Of course, my assessment is so much like those of so many others. We are forever deciding that what people will be in the future will be just like what they have been in the past. Jesus seemed to look at a person and see what the potential was, and He called on people to become the potential that He saw in them. The identity of any person is wrapped up in his name. Jesus sought to give Simon a new name because He saw the potential for Simon to be a *solid rock* rather than a *flittering dove.* To name a person is in a sense to call him into being, and that is what Jesus was doing with Simon. He was calling *Rock* into existence.

A rock is not the prettiest thing in the world, even if it is a diamond in the rough. A rock isn't fancy, and it has no finesse. If a rock gets rolling in the wrong direction, watch out! Who knows what destruction or obstruction it can cause. Of course, it also is true that once a rock settles down, it pretty much stays in place. So Jesus called Simon "Rock," and it was a name that stuck with him for the rest of his life.

Simon had been around Jesus all this time, and finally some of what Jesus had been saying was beginning to sink in. What satisfaction and relief Jesus must have had! All of His effort had not been in vain. Someone was finally catching on to who He was and what He was about. Peter was moving on up. He had been a fisherman and Jesus had invited him to become a fisher of men. Now, with this new insight percolating in Simon, Jesus renamed him and moved him on up to be the keeper of the keys of the kingdom. Peter had been promoted.

The Expectation of Discipleship

Everything that Jesus told Peter was not blessedness. As a matter-of-fact, some of what He said sounded more like a curse than like a blessing. Jesus urged His disciples not to tell anybody that He was the Messiah. Then He proceeded to tell them that being Messiah would involve a lot of heartache, suffering, pain, and eventually death. Well, Peter couldn't take such a negative attitude. He believed in the power of positive thinking—even if it were wrong. Peter told Jesus, "You're crazy! All of this pain, suffering, and death You are talking about is not going to happen. Hey, You've got us; You've got me. Good old Rocky, remember?" (author's paraphrase).

Maybe that is just what Jesus did remember, and that is why Jesus lit into him. If you have never thought of Jesus being angry except when He cleansed the Temple, how do you read His command to Peter, "Get behind Me, Satan!" I have never heard anyone called the devil in a kind and delightful tone. I certainly don't think Jesus was being mild and soft spoken when He said this to Peter. Peter was a rock, but this time he was an obstructor, which is what the word *Satan* means. Now the rock was in the way, attempting to block the path that the Messiah, the Son of God, was going to take.

What a reversal Peter's action took! Here in two paragraphs in Matthew's Gospel, the rock rolled from the peak of insight to the pit of darkness. How could he be so sharp one moment and so dull the next?

One of the reasons we like to berate Peter for flip-flopping is because it keeps the focus away from us. When was the most recent time you rolled from the peak of insight to the pit of darkness? Was it last week, yesterday, or this morning? When did you last roll your life out in front of Christ and seek to block His way because you were convinced He was off track in this willingness to suffer and even lay down His life to show the love of God?

There were other times when Peter said the wrong thing, got the wrong point, or did the wrong thing. On one occasion Jesus was talking about forgiveness, and Peter wanted so much to receive Jesus' approval. This desire seems so transparent in Peter. Maybe I see it so clearly because the need for approval is so much a part of me. In any case, Peter tried to get the jump on Jesus. On more than one occasion, Peter had heard Jesus talk about forgiveness. He knew from experience that forgiveness was Jesus' forte. This time Peter initiated the conversation about forgiveness because he wanted to impress Jesus with his insight and his bigheartedness. So Peter asked Jesus a question, "If somebody keeps on sinning against me, how many times do I have to forgive him?" (AP).

The question gave away Peter's attitude. He saw forgiveness as a demand, a requirement rather than a natural outgrowth of love and concern for the one who wronged him. Peter also revealed his attitude by answering his own question. He was not really looking for or expecting an answer. Peter wanted Jesus to confirm what he already thought. Peter thought that to forgive someone seven times would be the limit. Perhaps Peter thought that since seven was the perfect number to forgive someone, seven times would be perfect forgiveness.

Jesus responded by saying that if we forgave someone seventy-seven times or seven times seventy times (variant texts of Matt. 18:22 give both numbers), we are just getting warmed up. Keeping score denies forgiveness to another and betrays a lack of the authentic spirit of forgiveness. The numbers Jesus used were His way of expressing the infinity of forgiveness, like the psalmist had done by saying "as far as the east is from the west, so far does he remove our transgressions from us" (Ps. 103:12). Jesus reversed the law of vengence expressed by Lamech (Gen. 4:23-24) which was endless revenge. In contrast to this, the disciple of Christ is to practice endless forgiveness. Forgiveness toward others is to be limitless, just as the love of God is limitless.

Peter expressed another form of denial in his experience on the mountain of transfiguration. Peter, James, and John were with Jesus on the mountain, and a change came over Jesus. As they observed Jesus, they also saw Moses and Elijah talking with Jesus. This was an ecstatic worship experience for all three of them. Mark (9:6) and Luke (9:33) wrote that they did not know what to say. But as often was the case, Peter said something. He suggested to Jesus that they build three tabernacles—dwelling places—and just stay on the mountain. As with any mountaintop experiences, the temptation often is to remain on the mountain. One might call this the three-tabernacle syndrome. If one could just stay on the mountain of ecstasy one would not have to journey into the valley of struggle, hurt, misery, and despair. Peter wanted to do more than just savor the moment. He wanted to institutionalize it. He wanted to freeze the experience and bask in its warmth forever. This was a high worship experience for Peter, James, and John. We, like they, need to encounter the living God in worship and have mountaintop experiences in our lives. However, we must not deny the existence of the valley and our responsibility to journey into the valley.

It is important to notice what Jesus did when Peter suggested the building of tabernacles. Jesus did not say anything. They encountered

God announcing that this was His beloved Son with whom He was well pleased. Jesus touched them, told them not to be afraid, and then He started walking down the valley. He gave no verbal response to Peter's tabernacle question. He simply led them down from the mountaintop of worship into the valley of ministry. The Synoptic Gospels record the account of the transfiguration and the healing of a demon-possessed boy back to back.

In a magnificent painting, Raphael has combined these two events. In the left-hand corner, Raphael depicted Christ as He received light and power from God and as He talked with Elijah and Moses with the three disciples looking on in awe. In the same painting on the right-hand side are the images of the distressed father, the demon-possessed boy, and the frustrated disciples who could not bring about healing. In one frame this picture holds together the double focus of worship and ministry, the mountaintop and the valley. Numerous times the temptation avails itself to the followers of Christ to seize some moment of glory and by so doing to deny the struggles, pain, doubts, and suffering that also are part of discipleship. Always the mountain of worship is more enjoyable than the daily ministry or the way of the cross. Keeping these two in balance is difficult but essential. Jesus very effectively responded redemptively to the denial of Peter by leading the disciples down from the mountain of worship into the valley of ministry.

Later on, Peter was around when Jesus and the rich ruler discussed the essentials of eternal life. The disciples were amazed at what Jesus said about it being easier for a camel to go through the eye of a needle than for a rich person to enter the kingdom of heaven. Of course, Jesus was suggesting that what was essential was to let nothing get between the person and his relationship with God. Here is where Peter spoke up again stating that he and the other disciples had given up everything to be Jesus' disciples. Peter wondered what they would get out of following Jesus. Isn't that the question every follower of Christ asks at some point in the journey? What is in this for me? When Peter asked that, Jesus really took it pretty easy on him. In other ways and at other times Jesus had said: what is in this for My disciples and for Me is a cross. Basically, Jesus told Peter that he would get plenty of life and worth out of following Him, so would everybody else. Jesus left it at that for the time being.

The Climactic Denial

Then there was the time when Jesus and His disciples were eating supper together, the last time. Jesus started to wash the disciples' feet, and Peter denied Jesus the opportunity to wash his feet. He said, "Oh no! Don't wash my feet" (AP). Jesus explained that they were part of each other and servants together. To wash their feet represented the bonding of servants of God. Then Peter burst out, "Well then, what are You waiting for? Wash my feet, my hands, and my head" (AP). Peter was forever vacillating from one extreme to the other. First he didn't want Jesus washing his feet. Then he wanted Jesus to give him a bath (see John 10:8-9).

At the same meal Jesus said that He would be leaving them soon. Peter didn't get the point, so he asked about it. Jesus said that no one could follow Him. Peter wondered why he couldn't follow. Then Jesus said the most painful thing that Peter ever heard Him say to him. "Truly, I say to you, this very night, before the cock crows, you will deny me three times" (Matt. 26:34). That was such a difficult thing for Peter to hear that he denied that he would ever deny Jesus. Peter just could not believe what he had heard Jesus say.

Denial is a common coping mechanism that we human beings use to avoid facing and dealing with issues and events that are painful. One common method of denial is to sleep. A person who is depressed is one who does not or cannot face the reality of life and thus seeks to withdraw from life. Sleep is one of the methods of withdrawal. In the garden of Gethsemane is one of Peter's more blatant forms of denial. After Jesus and His disciples had shared a meal together, Peter had rushed to assure Jesus that even if everybody else forsook Him, he would not. Apparently, all of the disciples except Judas went to Gethsemane with Jesus (Matt. 26:36).

Jesus invited Peter, James, and John to go on further with Him. Then He asked them to remain and watch with Him. Jesus went on further. Jesus obviously was in agony. He was troubled and seeking comfort. He needed His disciples to watch with Him. He especially needed the support of those who had been closest to Him. He wanted and needed them to bear His burden with Him. But what happened? While He went on further to pray in solitude, Peter, James, and John went to sleep. When Jesus returned, He sought to respond to their denial by asking them if they could not stay awake for one hour. He urged them to watch and pray, so they might not enter into temptation. Jesus was preparing Himself for what He sensed was coming. He sought to get His disciples to prepare themselves, but it was too painful. They preferred to avoid the painful thoughts of what might happen, so they went to sleep. This was the perfect, passive form of denial.

I wonder what would have happened had Peter and the others remained awake, watched, and prayed. Would they have been better prepared to face the events that came? Would Peter have been less eager to resort to violence when the arrest came? Would Peter have been more willing to stand up for Jesus in the courtyard of the high priest? As painful and burdensome as life was becoming for Jesus, He sought to prepare Himself in communion with God. In the face of the burden and pain that Peter sensed Jesus was experiencing, Peter went to sleep. It was more than he was willing to face. The pain was too intense. Thus he went to sleep. That was the easiest way Peter knew to deny what was happening. He preferred to cope that way rather than to watch and pray. When the worst came only hours later, Peter was unprepared to deal with it, and his denial became aggressive, even more blatant than his sleeping in Gethsemane. When Jesus needed the support and care of those closest to Him, they were asleep. It was a strong hint of the lack of support He would receive from them in the hours to come.

Later that evening while they were in the garden of Gethsemane, the soldiers came to arrest Jesus. Once again, Peter sought to be the obstructor. He attempted to deny what was taking place by using violence to keep violence from happening. Peter jerked out his sword and took off Malchus's ear. I don't know if that was a warning blow of what was to come, or if Peter was just off the mark with his sword as he had been so often with his statements. Jesus responded to this denial by telling Peter to put the sword away and to quit getting in the way of His being the Messiah, the Son of the living God.

Peter followed Jesus along with an unnamed disciple to the courtyard of the high priest. Through the influence of the unnamed disciple, Peter was permitted access to the courtyard. A maid thought she recognized Peter and asked if he were not one of Jesus' disciples. Peter was evasive saying, "I do not know what you mean" (Matt. 26:70). Peter moved closer to the fire. He had never been so cold in his entire life. Another maid asked him the same question. This time with an oath Peter replied, "I do not know the man" (Matt. 26:72). Then some bystanders, who had been overhearing, chided Peter suggesting that his accent had given him away. But Peter denied knowing Jesus again. With each denial,Peter seemed to feel colder and moved closer to the fire.

Then there was a sound that unlocked an avalanch of memories in Peter's mind. As some rooster crowed at the rising sun, Peter remembered denying that he would deny Jesus, but now he had denied Him three times. How unglued Peter must have felt, and then there was one more devastating experience. About that time, Jesus was brought across the courtyard and He turned and looked at Peter (Luke 22:61). Oh the pained expression that must have been in Jesus' eyes as His eyes met Peter's! He had heard the voice of a close friend say, "I've never seen this guy before" (AP). With one look, Jesus responded to Peter's denial. For some reason I suspect that Jesus' look was a redemptive one. I think this because of Peter's reaction. Peter went out and wept bitterly (Luke 22:62). The tears poured down Peter's face like rain washing down a rock.

Can you imagine what it must have been like for Peter to see Jesus on the cross? Think of the remorse he felt. Think of the beating Peter gave himself for having failed so miserably. The chances are good that if he had been arrested with Jesus that Peter would have defended Him faithfully. Who of us cannot imagine circumstances where we know that we would be faithful to Christ? But situations in life never develop quite like we have played them out in our minds. Events in Jesus' life did not develop as Peter imagined. Never in his worst nightmares did Peter ever dream that he would deny Christ, although as I have sought to point out, denial was one of Peter's primary coping mechanisms throughout his encounters with Jesus. When conflict became most intense in Jesus' life, Peter denied the conflict.

The Redemptive Reunion

There is much tragedy in this story, but tragedy is not the end of the story. The Gospel writers record that after the resurrection of Jesus, the women were instructed to tell the disciples and Peter about the resurrection, as if Peter no longer considered himself one of the group. On Easter morning, the Denied and the denier met. Exactly what was said only they knew, and neither of them told. However, their last conversation on earth is recorded in the Gospel of John (John 21:15-19).

On the beach at daybreak, they talked. Some of the other disciples were there, and Jesus cooked breakfast for them. When they were finished eating, Jesus said, "Simon, son of John," because it seems if ever He meant business this was it, "do you love Me?" Peter said he did. Jesus asked the same question again, and then again. In all He asked the question three times to make up for the three times in the courtyard of the high priest. Then Jesus said, "Feed my lambs." "Tend my sheep" (vv. 15-16). I get the feeling that Peter was delighted to know that forgiveness was not limited to seven times. I also sense that this time, Peter didn't miss the point Jesus was making. In essence, Jesus promoted Peter to shepherd. He had come from being a fisher of fish, to a fisher of people, to keeper of the keys to the Kingdom, to a shepherd.

Out of this struggling, growing, agonizing relationship, Jesus continued to respond redemptively to Peter's denials. The result was that Peter became the leader of the early church. He was leader of the early church in Jerusalem for the first fifteen years after Jesus' resurrection. Denial continued to be Peter's major coping mechanism but to a lesser degree. It seems that the longer Peter lived in association with Christ and the more the Spirit of Christ dwelt in him, the more suspicious Peter became of the barriers that separated Jews from the rest of the people of the world. The deeper Peter plunged into the truth that he found in Christ, the more unwilling Peter was to confine himself to the artificial boundaries of Judaism.

Out of this growing awareness that Christ sought to tear down the barriers that separate people, Peter met Cornelius. What a contrast these two were! They were about the last two people anyone would ever expect to be drawn together and to accept each other. Cornelius was a Gentile, and Peter a Jew. Cornelius was a high-ranking officer, a man of the world, and a professional. Peter had no rank; he was a country boy and a laborer. Cornelius had an increasing sense of insufficiency in his religious life. Peter had a growing dissatisfaction with the institutionalism of Judaism. When Peter and Cornelius met, it was as though a great wall was once and for all removed.

Cornelius was the first Gentile publicly and officially welcomed into the fellowship of Christians without requiring conformity to the requirements of Jewish law. Peter's own words described the new awareness.

> You yourselves know how unlawful it is for a Jew to associate with or to visit any one of another nation; but God has shown me that I should not call any man common or unclean. . . . Truly I perceive that God shows no partiality, but in every nation any one who fears him and does what is right is acceptable to him (Acts 10:28, 34-35).

Later on Peter waffled on the issue of eating with the Gentiles. He received pressure from Paul for not eating with them. Then after Peter ate with Gentiles, he was pressured by the Jerusalem church for doing so. Vacillation was still a part of Peter's personality, but what a positive contribution he made to the development and life of the church. He traveled to other parts of the world and shared the gospel (1 Cor. 9:5). Later, Peter probably made a trip to Rome where he continued to share the gospel, and eventually was martyred for his commitment to God. At least, that is how church tradition claims Peter's life ended.

Peter often overestimated his own ability, underestimated the power of evil, and at times ignored the power of God. As a result Peter made mistakes, many of which were the result of his attempting to cope with his inadequacies and insecurities by denying that they existed. Jesus forgave Peter for his mistakes and his denials. Eventually, the church forgave Peter too, and he came to have a prominent place in the early life of the church. Jesus saw in Simon—*flittering dove* —the potential to become Peter—*solid rock.* Jesus kept calling Peter to become who and what he had the potential to be. Jesus continued to respond redemptively to Peter's denials until, eventually, Peter the rock became a real gem as a result of his willingness to allow the Master Jeweler to love him, labor with him, confront him, forgive him, and redeem him.

The story of Peter comes close to everyone who ever failed; therefore, it comes close to everyone. Who of us has not failed? Is not the story of Peter of such value to us because we see so much of ourselves in him? Are we not all deniers? Do we not spend much energy denying that we would ever deny Christ? Then some rooster crows somewhere, or someone's eyes penetrate ours, and we know that they are the eyes of Christ, so we go out and weep bitterly. We too are rocks, not always the solid, sturdy kind and yet not gems. Often we are the obstructor kind of rock that blocks the path of Christ. But never does God throw us on the heap of worthless stones.

As with Peter, so it is with us. God is seeking to work out the first Peter principle. God wants to take us from fishing for whatever to where He can get us into ministering to people, promote us to keepers of the keys of the kingdom, and, finally, to make us shepherds. That seems to be the way that God responds redemptively to denial. Will you allow God to redeem you from your denials? It is His work to turn a rock into a gem.

Note

1. John Claypool. "Simon Peter Revisited," Sermon delivered at Northminister Baptist Church, Jackson, Mississippi, 4 Jan. 1981, p. 2.

7
Responding to Betrayal

Matthew 26: 14-25, 47-56; 27: 3-9

Is there anything to a name? What about your name? What does it mean? Whenever you are asked: "Who are you?" how do you respond? Do you give your name and let that suffice, or do you add facts and feelings to help the inquirer know who you are? Names have significance for us because they are used to identify items and people within the world. Names help to give order to what without them would be a chaotic conglomeration.

In the creation narrative in Genesis, Adam was encouraged to name the animals. This was part of the creative process, and the animals were named according to the nature Adam saw in them (Gen. 2:19). This process helped the creation to have some order to it for Adam. There was a sense in which naming the animals was part of the process of human beings having control and dominion over the earth and what dwelled on the earth.

As the Old Testament suggested, names were an important part of the development of the Hebrew people. Names were given to people and places. Inherent in each name was something of the nature of that person or place. The name of Jacob meant *supplanter* and showed itself in the way he treated Esau. It was remembered that Jacob was born holding on to his twin brother's heel. Bethel meant *house of God,* and was given to a place Jacob designated to worship God because of his encounter with God there.

In biblical thought, a name is more than a label of identification. It is an expression of the essential nature of the one named. In Hebrew

123

thought, nothing exists unless it has a name. The promise of God that His people's name shall remain was a pledge that their existence would continue.

The name of a person says more about his or her parents than it says about the individual. A name may reveal dreams, expectations, and hopes that parents had for the child at birth. A name may have family or historical significance, and that may have an effect on the person if he is expected to fulfill the role that his name represents. Many names are popular because of the reputation developed by the better-known persons who had those names—such as David, Deborah, Mary, Elizabeth, John, or Peter. Other names seldom, if ever, are used because of the negative characteristics associated with them. Very few people have been named Absalom, Jezebel, Ananias, or Sapphira. Do you know anyone named Brutus or Benedict Arnold? What about Judas? No one is ever cursed with the name of Judas other than to indicate that someone has betrayed another.

The Gospel writers, writing thirty or more years after the ministry of Jesus, so clearly identified Judas as a betrayer that the name and betrayal became synonymous. Those writers hung the words, "the one who betrayed Jesus," around Judas's name like a signboard. As a result, a reader of the Gospels has a negative response and attitude toward Judas the very moment that he is introduced.

As we read the New Testament, we envision Judas as the villain. Certainly, there is no denying that he betrayed Jesus. I would never suggest that such a wrong be overlooked or discounted. However, we may have developed such disdain for Judas as a defense mechanism to keep ourselves from examining the ways and times that we are kinfolks with Judas.

Who Was Judas?

Judas Iscariot has to be the most enigmatic person in the Gospel story, if not in the entire Bible. The background and character of Judas as well as the meaning of his name, his motive for betraying Jesus, and the manner of his death all remain unsolvable riddles.

John's Gospel identified Judas as the son of Simon Iscariot. A variety of interpretations have been given to the meaning of Judas's name. It has been interpreted as assassin, man from Sychar, man of Issachar, man from Jericho, carrier of the leather bag, false one, liar, or hypocrite. At least one scholar has suggested that Judas was the brother of Mary, Martha, and Lazarus.[1] The most common interpretation of Judas's name is that Iscariot identified him as a man from Kerioth. If this were true, then Judas was the only one of the twelve apostles who was from Judea. The other eleven were Galileans.

It is to the credit of the early church that it told Judas's story at all. His actions were such a black mark against the followers of Jesus that they must have had a great struggle to mention Judas's name in any context. His actions were too hot to handle, and I'm sure there were those who would have liked to have dropped Judas from the story completely. But the church refused to do that. However, all of the Gospel writers do list Judas last in their orders of the apostles.

Jesus chose Judas like He chose His other disciples. He invited them to follow Him. He invited each of them to be with Him and to be sent out by Him to preach and to be given the authority to cast out demons (Mark 3:14-15). Jesus saw potential and possibilities in Judas like He saw them in every person He invited to follow Him. There is every reason to believe that Judas responded to Jesus' invitation with every bit as much enthusiasm as any of the other disciples.

Apparently, Judas found acceptance among the apostles. He became treasurer of the group. Regardless of how that came about, holding the position indicated a certain amount of trust placed in him by his colleagues. John (12:6) suggested that Judas was dishonest and embezzled money from the group's treasury. However, at the time seemed to have had any such suspicions of Judas. At the time when Jesus dropped the bombshell that one of them would betray Him, none in the group blamed Judas. Even when Judas left the group meeting soon after that, no one suspected anything except that perhaps Judas was going on an errand for Jesus (John 13:29). Judas was a card-carrying apostle for as long as any of the twelve. He was with

Jesus and learned from Him as a disciple for the three years of Jesus' public ministry.

Betrayal by Judas

Judas betrayed Jesus. Apparently, he told the chief priests and officers where Jesus could be located. Judas knew the routine of the apostles and Jesus. It must have been fairly common for them to go to the garden of Gethsemane. The religious leaders were interested in taking Jesus in a place and at a time that would not arouse the public's suspicion or wrath. Jesus' popularity had been increasing continually. Opinion polls ran heavily in favor of Him. They were higher than ever after His cleansing of the Temple because those who had been gouged by the buyers and sellers felt some justice finally had been done. Judas fitted the needs of the religious leaders. He could and did give them information about when and where they could capture Jesus away from the crowd.

Judas led the leaders to Jesus. Matthew and Mark indicated that Judas had arranged a sign with those who came to take Jesus. The one Judas kissed would be Jesus. Luke made much out of the kiss of betrayal (22:47-48). John, however, indicated that when they came for Jesus that Jesus was so in control, all Judas could do was stand by and watch (18:1-12). He was useless at that point. How Judas pointed out Jesus to those who wanted to arrest him is not as significant as the fact that Judas helped hasten the end for Jesus by revealing to His enemies where they could take Him with the most ease and the least resistance.

Why Judas betrayed Jesus is not nearly as clear as the method Judas used. There are a number of possible motives for Judas's betrayal. Judas was more like us than anything else in the world. He was a human being. Judas operated from a variety of mixed motives. Who of us does anything solely from one motive?

A few people have suggested that Judas turned Jesus over to the authorities for the money. These people have suggested that Judas was a person who could not or would not resist an opportunity for personal gain. Part of their basis for this is John's comment mentioned above about Judas dipping his hand into the till. But thirty pieces of silver, equivalent to about fifteen dollars today, seems hardly enough to support the idea that Judas betrayed Jesus only for the money he could get out of the deed.

Others suggest that Judas was somewhat of a loner or at least felt lonely being the only Judean in this group of Galileans. And it seems quite plausible that Judas suffered from the concerns about the pecking order of the disciples as did some of the others, namely James and John. There is every reason to believe, from the psychological side of the matter, that each of the apostles wrestled with the issue of who was most important or who had the most power in the group. Such wrestling and struggling is a common part of group dynamics. There are those who think that Judas felt somewhat slighted or left out in some way in the group. So out of his anger and frustration, Judas sought to get back at Jesus, the leader of the group. Often when things do not go as a member of the group wants them to go, the leader gets the blame. Whether or not this action is justified is seldom, if ever, considered by those who do the blaming.

Of course, some people see Judas's action clearly as the will of God. These argue that it was part of God's plan of salvation for Jesus to die, and Judas was simply part of that overall plan. I'm not sure there are many people who want to worship a god like that although there is evidence that people will worship almost any kind of god. To say that Judas was doing the will of God is fatalistic. It also is to say that Judas really had no choice in the matter or to suggest that if Judas had not betrayed Jesus, he would have been going against the will of God. What an unfair position in which to put Judas! If Judas were doing God's will by betraying Jesus, then it makes no sense that later he killed himself. To suggest that Judas was doing God's will also makes God an accessory to the crime of betrayal and at least a coconspirator in the death of His own Son.

I offer one other explanation of Judas's action which is more plausible for me. The Jews had been maltreated for several hundred years by the occupied troops of Rome under a variety of leaders. They wanted their nation freed from this foreign police force which, depending upon the officer in charge, vacillated from maintaining order to extreme harassment, persecution, and making a mockery of what the Jews considered sacred. I doubt that many of us have any way of imagining what that would be like.

Maltreatment and persecution had occurred so much for the Jews that many of them would not take it any longer. They had revolted against Syria, who occupied Israel in the second century B.C. Led by Judas Maccabee, the revolution was known as the Maccabean Revolution. As a result of the Maccabean Revolution, there developed a climate for zealous commitment to overthrow foreign occupation troops and rid the land of them. Later, with Roman occupation, these ardent supporters of a Roman-free Israel became known as the Zealots.

All of Israel tied their hopes to a Messiah, a deliverer who would come, conquer Rome, and reestablish God's reign in the land. They built these hopes on a military model. They believed that this Messiah would be very much like King David. They believed this so much that they expected the Messiah to come from David's family.

The theology of zeal that motivated the Zealot originated in the exclusivistic worship of the one true God of Israel. This zeal was transferred to the law of God. The Zealot was the strict interpreter of the Law who was willing to follow the way of zeal for the law of the God of Israel unto death. The Zealot was willing not only to kill a Gentile or to lay down his life rather than transgress the Law, but also the Zealot was quite prepared to take the life of a fellow Israelite, if necessary, out of his zeal for the law of God. A Zealot tended to see his cause as a holy one. Once the Zealot justified his cause as holy, then any means became permissible to achieve the objective. This justification is expressed in a statement in Taylor Caldwell's novel *I, Judas* when one person comments about a leader:

And what of a leader? Without the Messiah there is not hope for a general uprising. All wait for the Deliverer and will not be delivered without him. If we do not find a Messiah, we will manufacture one.[2]

From what can be pieced together about Judas Iscariot, apparently he was very zealous about his people, their worship of God, and the removal of Roman forces, domination, and influence. There is no clear evidence that he was a member of the Zealot party as was his fellow apostle Simon the Zealot. Nevertheless, Judas was a man consumed with zeal. He pinned his hopes for the deliverance of his people on Jesus.

In a sense, Judas heard Jesus say what he wanted to hear. How often that is true of each of us. Some of Jesus' phrases and actions fitted exactly with Judas' beliefs and desires. Judas became a follower of Jesus. There is no evidence but that Judas was enthusiastic in this discipleship. He could hardly wait until the day when the great event would take place, but wait he did. A year passed. No army was being formed, but Jesus was gaining support. His popularity was increasing. At times Jesus spoke to and about issues that were on target from Judas' perspective.

Just as Judas would begin to get excited, Jesus would start talking about and relating to a blind man, a Samaritan woman, or permit a woman to waste an entire bottle of expensive perfume on His feet. Judas would become frustrated when Jesus seemed more concerned about individuals than about issues that affected many individuals. Judas was much more concerned about the blindness in government than he was about some man who had been blind from birth. Judas wanted something done about the way Rome was raping Israel, but Jesus seemed more interested in a woman caught in adultery. All of Israel was being crippled by occupation forces, and Jesus spent time asking a crippled man if he wanted to get well.

Into the second year of His ministry, more people were coming to listen to Jesus. In some places huge crowds gathered. At any moment, Jesus could have given the signal to rush the guards, but He never did.

Still there was no army, just a few more disciples than at the beginning.

Jesus entered the third year of His mission. He talked more about His kingdom. His language seemed to have a sterner, more intense, more forthright tone to it. Conflicts were on the increase as people questioned and disagreed with Jesus. There were numerous little confrontations that seemed to be leading to a major one. The timing for things seemed to be right on Palm Sunday when Jesus entered Jerusalem to streets lined with pilgrims shouting, "Hosanna." They laid palm branches in front of Him as if He were a king, a deliverer, the Messiah. But Jesus didn't do anything to try to organize or unite the people together into a revolutionary force.

He did go to the Temple and cleaned out the place. Was the tension ever thick! Then Jesus had acted like a Zealot when he drove out the money changers, and Judas remembered that the Scriptures said, "Zeal for thy house will consume me" (John 2:17). Judas must have thought that it could not be long now before Jesus led the revolution. Of course, Jesus already was leading a revolution, but it was so different from what Judas expected and understood as needing to be that Judas was dissatisfied with its prospects and possibilities. Things were not happening as Judas expected nor as rapidly as he thought they should.

Judas decided to help the cause along. He would force Jesus to play His hand. He would put Jesus in an uncompromising position where Jesus would be forced to act. Judas made a deal. The Jewish leaders wanted to do away with Jesus.

> "We must keep our eyes on this Jesus. He is more dangerous than the other" (a reference to John the Baptist). Gamaliel asked, "Why do you say that?" "Fanatics we can deal with. They thrive on emotion and that soon spends itself. But this one deals in reason and is mild and moderate. He wears better."[3]

To help the cause along, Judas agreed to turn Jesus in. He left the supper before the party was over although, according to Luke, not until they had shared the bread and wine (22:21). Judas led the way to the garden and told them to lay low until he gave the signal. He showed the soldiers the one to arrest by kissing him. The most common way for a disciple to greet his master was with a kiss. At least since the time that Judas kissed Jesus, the meaning of a kiss has been ambiguous. Is the kiss one receives a sign of affection, or is it the kiss of death? When they went to take Jesus, He did not resist.

How shocked Judas must have been! As John told about this, he had no kiss as the signal. John portrayed Jesus so much in control that Jesus asked who they wanted, and when they responded, He told them He was the one. (12:5). All Judas could do was stand, first on one foot, and then on the other, and watch. In his mind, Judas must have worked out how Jesus would react. He was convinced that if Jesus were forced to decide between being arrested and resisting, Jesus would resist. Judas had failed to learn that in other traps that had been laid for Jesus by the Pharisees, Jesus invariably responded with alternatives they had never considered. When they seized Jesus, He went with them, not so much reluctantly as much as though He were more in charge than they. Although they put the cuffs on Jesus, there was something about His attitude that seemed to disclose that He was the free one, and those taking Him were bound.

Judas was dumbfounded. He began to realize that if Jesus didn't do something, he was a goner. Judas took the money back. You'd think since Judas had done what he was paid to do that he would have taken the money and found some place to spend it. For some reason, Judas just wasn't in the mood. Before Judas could clear the cobwebs of confusion from his mind about what was happening and what he was going to do now, Jesus was on the cross.

Judas's response to what had taken place was to plunge into despair. In his despair, Judas killed himself (Matt. 27:3-9); Acts 1:18-19). Suicide is an act of despair in its ultimate form. Judas did not wait around to see what God could and would do with human defection. This was the greatest failure of Judas, greater than his betrayal, great as that was. This is the significant difference between Peter and Judas.

Peter's denial was a form of betrayal. When Peter realized what he had done, he wept bitterly. Peter repented to God because it was against God that he had sinned. Peter received forgiveness from God and acceptance by the disciples. Judas felt remorse over what he had done, and he went to his coconspirators to return the money. But they rejected the money and his remorse. They did not want the blood money nor the blood guilt. They used the money to buy a field. They had used Judas for what they wanted, and then they did not need him anymore. When they turned him away, Judas shut out all other alternatives. He never went to God to repent. He never sought out the disciples for help. The only alternative Judas sought was despair. He pursued it and killed himself. What a difference between Peter and Judas—the alternatives they sought and the results they experienced! Later, when the early church was writing all of this down, they listed Peter first in the order of the apostles and Judas last.

We Are Like Judas

It is instructive not only for us to learn *about* Judas but also for us to learn *from* him. In many ways we are more like Judas than Jesus. We really don't like to make such a confession, but it is true. Each of us has a shadow side, a seamy side, and a part to ourselves that we do not know; or, if we know it, we do not like what we see. We tend to project our shadow sides onto someone like Judas. One of the reasons that Judas so often has been portrayed as all bad is because we project onto him all that is evil in us and never confront it. Traitors have been treated with the greatest contempt because deep within people there is that same potential to be traitors. We believe that if we destroy traitors and betrayers, we somehow destroy that part of ourselves that would betray. There is nothing in Judas and what he did that is not common to each of us.

Just as individuals have shadow sides, so do groups, organizations, and nations. Is not much of the hatred that many whites feel for blacks fueled by the projection by whites of their shadow sides onto blacks. What about the religious war in Ireland between the Protestants and the Catholics? Do they not represent each other's shadow side? This is also true between nations. Consider the relationship between the United States and the Soviet Union. We are diametrically opposed to each other philosophically, politically, and economically. Do we not represent each other's shadow side? Did not President Reagan verbalize that when he referred to the Soviet Union as an evil empire? The shadow sides of these two nations receive so much emphasis that reality is distorted; the enemies become so frightened of their own shadows that they see no alternative actions other than what they are presently doing which is escalating fear and escalating the development of nuclear arms. Such action breeds despair, and the despair leads to suicide, the suicide of the entire human species as well as the entire earth that God has created.

On a more personal basis, how are you like Judas? How do you betray Christ? I know you want to yell and scream at me that you don't betray Christ, and maybe you ought to do that right now. Now that you have screamed at me, let's look at some of the reasons why we betray Jesus.

Greed is out of the question. We cannot sell information about Jesus. More books have been written about Jesus than any other person in history. Information is easily accessible about the Nazarene. We claim that we cannot sell information about Jesus, but we often use Jesus to sell ourselves or the products we want others to buy. Often it is expedient for us to use religion to our advantage. If we drop the name of Jesus here and there, people may respond more positively to us. Many people trust religious folks, at least those who sound religious, more than other folks. Our motives for telling where Christ is may be our greed for approval, acceptance, or the meeting of some other personal need.

Sometimes we betray Christ because we have become disillusioned with God. We develop our expectations of God, and we are determined that God will fit into our mold. We expect life to move in a specific direction. When it does not, we begin to wonder why. We often see ourselves as the exemptions to the problems, struggles, and difficulties of life. We assume that we deserve some special exemption because of our fervent zeal and devotion to God. We function on the premise that we ought to be paid for doing whatever good we are doing. When the rewards we receive are in the forms of struggle and pain that are shaped into a cross, then we become disillusioned with God. When God's ways fail to be our ways, we become angry and embittered.

Often Christ does not turn out to be the Christ we expected or wanted. We want Christ to confirm what we already believe and to baptize our present actions as right. We do not want Christ challenging us to alter or change. If Christ will not be the kind of Messiah we want Him to be, we will sell Him for whatever price we can get.

When was the last time you sought to force Christ into action? Who of us has not attempted to bargain with God? We want God to function on our schedules, and we seek to manipulate God to do our bidding. We make conditional promises thinking that we can maneuver God into doing things for us because of our promise of devotion to Him. Who of us has not said at least once, "Lord, if You will get me out of this situation, I will change my ways and live more like You want me to live."

Betrayal is a harsh word. It describes Judas. It describes some other people we know. Whether we like it or not, betrayal also describes us. We are more like Judas than Jesus. The tragedy of betrayal is that betrayal convinces us that we know better than God how to deal with ourselves. Let us learn from Judas and not give ourselves over to despair. Let us give ourselves over to God and discover what God can and will do with human defection. The greatest failure of Judas was that he shut the door on the alternative of what God could and would do with his repentance. Despair, he felt, was his only option, and it led to suicide—despair in its ultimate form.

Jesus' Response to Betrayal

Have you ever been betrayed? How did you feel? What action did you take? What action would you have liked to have taken toward your betrayer? When I have been betrayed, I have reacted with anger. I have wanted to take revenge on the person. I have thought of and sought ways to get even with the one who has betrayed me. Someone needs to settle the score, and I want the satisfaction of doing it.

How do you think Jesus responded to being betrayed? Naturally, He was angered by Judas' betrayal. Examination of Jesus' responses to Judas will be instructive for us on how to respond redemptively to betrayal.

One of the sternest statements that Jesus made to Judas was at the time that Mary anointed Jesus' feet with expensive perfume. This event occurred in the context of Jesus having brought Lazarus, Mary's brother, back to life. As a response of gratitude and as an indication that Mary was becoming aware of the terrible price that Jesus would pay for being the kind of Messiah He had chosen to be, Mary poured a bottle of expensive perfume on Jesus' feet. Judas responded that the money would have been better spent if it had been given to the poor. Judas's response revealed a form of betrayal. He was not willing to allow Jesus to be the kind of Messiah that Jesus wanted to be. To be a Messiah who was interested in individuals and to fail to see the practicalities of the efficient use of money was unacceptable to Judas.

Jesus strongly rebuked Judas. "Let her alone, let her keep it for the day of my burial. The poor you always have with you, but you do not always have me" (John 12:7-8). Judas probably heard Jesus saying "If you had seen one starving peasant you had seen them all." That was not what Jesus was saying. Jesus was not being insensitive, but His statement was disturbing then, and it continues to disturb people today. What does it mean? Certainly, Jesus was not suggesting that God made some people poor or that some people are just destined to be poor and hungry. Rather, Jesus' statement is an indictment that people have refused to adopt and practice God's economic policy. If we were generous and free from addiction to material things, then there would be no poor among us. Since we still have the poor with us, we have failed because we have fallen short of God's radical generosity. The poor are still with us because we have been tightfisted rather than openhanded.

Jesus' statement that we always have the poor with us was a confrontive, redemptive word. It was an attempt by Jesus to respond to Judas's betrayal and to warn all of His followers that they should be struggling with the great sickness in human beings which was dragging Jesus to His death rather than trying to cover one corner of the symptoms by glibly offering to spend somebody else's money. Jesus' confrontation of Judas was an attempt to shake Judas awake to the kind of Messiah Jesus came to be.

Later on, Jesus was eating His last supper with His disciples. He shocked them by announcing that one of them was going to betray Him. It is to their credit that they asked, "Lord, is it I?" rather than pointing accusing fingers at each other and attempting to pin the blame on someone. The response of the apostles also indicates that none of Judas's actions or words to this point had raised any of their suspicions about him. It was at this point in the meal that Jesus made a very strong statement. He said, "It would have been better for that man if he had not been born" (Matt. 26:24). This was a difficult word to hear. It is a troubling word to hear now. Jesus was saying that it would have been better never to have been born than to do such a dastardly deed as to betray Him. Wasn't Jesus confronting Judas and by so doing opening the door to him to make another choice or to change his mind before the deed was done? Jesus was reaching out to Judas by attempting to show him how terrible was the deed of betrayal. Judas responded by asking, "Is it I, Master?" (Matt. 26:25). Jesus answered, "You have said so." (Matt. 26:25) This may have been a colloquial expression for yes. It could also have been the way Jesus said to Judas the options are still open. No matter how far you have gone down the path of betrayal, you can stop now and turn around.

This seems to be what John conveyed in his account of Jesus' prediction of His betrayal. He was at supper with the disciples. Peter tried to get John to get Jesus to tell them who the betrayer was. Apparently, John was on Jesus' right, and Judas was on His left. Jesus said whoever dipped his bread in the bowl with Him was the one. All of them had dipped in the bowl together from time to time. In that sense all of them betrayed Jesus.

But Jesus sought a private rather than public exposure of Judas. He dipped His bread and gave it to Judas. As Jesus looked longingly into Judas's eyes, he said, "Decide now. Make your decision, and do whatever you are going to do" (author's paraphrase) Here was confrontation, challenge, and invitation. Jesus sought to allow Judas space to change his mind and come back to Him. Apparently, none of the other eleven suspected what Judas might do because John wrote that when Judas left the room they thought he was going on an errand for Jesus.

Surely one of the most stinging indictments ever uttered happened earlier in Jesus' relationship with His apostles. He said that He had chosen the twelve of them to be with Him, and yet one of them was a devil (John 6:70-71). It is troubling to read that Jesus called Judas a devil. Of course, Jesus also called Peter Satan (Mark 8:33). Two of the twelve were singled out as emissaries of the evil one. Both stood together at the outset under that damning indictment, but the outcome of their lives could not have been more different. Peter became the chief apostle, and Judas died a tragic suicide. Jesus accused both of them and yet did everything possible to break the tempter's power. The opposite responses of these two men to the same predicament show that human free will was a crucial factor in their decisions about who Jesus was and how they would relate to Him.

Jesus responded to betrayal by reaching out to Judas. Jesus confronted, challenged, and invited Judas to change directions. It really seems that Judas was so bent on making Jesus fit his image of the Messiah that he refused to let Jesus shape him in His image. Yet even to the end of His life, Jesus was still trying to reach Judas.

One day a man was swimming laps. When he stopped, a man in the next lane said, "You don't stop, do you?" To which the first man replied, "Not until I'm finished." That was the approach that Jesus took in responding to the betrayal of Judas. Jesus did not stop until

He was finished. He was never finished in reaching out to Judas until His life was ended. May we who are more like Judas than Jesus learn from Judas's greatest failure, and may we accept the confrontations, the challenges, and the invitations that Jesus offers us that will bring us back from the brink of despair to which our betrayals have taken us.

Notes

1. F. W. Gingrich, "Judas," *The Interpreter's Dictionary of the Bible* (Nashville: Abingdon Press, 1962), vol. 2, p. 1007.

2. Taylor Caldwell and Jess Stearn, *I, Judas* (New York: Atheneum Press, 1977), p. 36. Used by permission.

3. Ibid., p. 91.

Bibliography

Books

Allen, Clifton J., ed. *The Broadman Bible Commentary*. Nashville: Broadman Press, 1969.

Barclay, William. *The Daily Study Bible Series*. Edinburgh: The Saint Andrew Press, 1958.

_____. *The Mind of Jesus*. New York: Harper Brothers, 1960.

Buechner, Frederick. *Peculiar Treasures: A Biblical Who's Who*. New York: Harper and Row, Publishers, 1979.

_____. *Wishful Thinking: A Theological ABC*. San Francisco: Harper and Row, Publishers, 1975.

Buttrick, George A. Editor. *The Interpreter's Dictionary of the Bible*. Nashville: Abingdon Press, 1962.

Caldwell, Taylor and Jess Stearn. *I, Judas*. New York: Atheneum Press, 1977.

Campbell, Ernest. *Locked in a Room with Open Doors*. Waco: Word Books, Inc., 1974.

Jordan, Clarence. *The Cotton Patch Version of Luke and Acts*. New York: Association Press, 1969.

Kittel, Gerhard and Gerhard Friedrich. *Theological Dictionary of the New Testament*. Grand Rapids: William B. Eerdmans Publishing Company, 1964.

Lester, Andrew D. *Coping with Your Anger: A Christian Guide*. Philadelphia: The Westminster Press, 1983.

Mace, David. *Love and Anger in Marriage.* Grand Rapids: The Zondervan Corporation, 1982.

Menninger, Karl, MD; Martin Mayman; and Paul Pruyser. *The Vital Balance.* New York: The Viking Press, 1963.

Moyer, Kenneth E. *The Physiology of Hostility.* Chicago: Markham Press, 1971.

Nouwen, Henri J. M. *The Wounded Healer: Ministry in Contemporary Society.* Garden City, New York: Doubleday and Company, 1972.

Peck, Scott M. *The Road Less Traveled: A New Psychology of Love, Traditional and Spiritual Growth.* New York: Simon and Schuster, 1978.

Robertson, A. T. *Word Pictures in the New Testament.* Nashville: Sunday School Board of the SBC, 1930.

Sayers, Dorothy L. *Are Women Human?* Grand Rapids: William B. Eerdmans Publishing Company, 1971.

Schell, Jonathan. *The Fate of the Earth.* New York: Alfred A. Knopf, 1982.

Smyth, John. *Paralleles, Censures, Observations.*

Southard, Samuel. *Anger in Love.* Philadelphia: The Westminster Press, 1973.

Tennyson, Alfred Lloyd. *The Poems of Tennyson.* Cambridge: The Riverside Press, 1898.

Webster's New World Dictionary College Edition. New York: The World Publishing Company, 1964.

Wink, Walter. *Transforming Bible Study.* Nashville: Abingdon Press, 1980.

Periodicals

Fore, William F. "Religion and Television: Report on the Research." *The Christian Century* 101, no. 23, 18-25 July 1984.

Mace, David. "Love, Anger, and Intimacy." *Proceedings of the 1979 Christian Life Commission Seminar on Help for Families.* Nashville: Broadman Press, 1979.

Steele, David. "Moses Gets the Nod, Then Exits." *Theology Today* XLI, no. 3, October 1984.

Unpublished Sermon

Claypool, John. "Simon Peter Revisited." Sermon delivered at North-minster Baptist Church, Jackson, Mississippi, January 4, 1981.